# Catching the American Dream®

# *Entrepreneurial Marketing*

**Jim and Jo Ann Carland**

A Whitney Press Publication

# CONTENTS

# About the Authors

This book was written by two people who have been there. It is not filled with theories and blue sky. It is a down to earth, practical, hands on approach. It is readable and filled with anecdotes and illustrations which add up to make it an enjoyable book which is both informative and easy to read.

Jo Ann and Jim Carland are uniquely suited to write about entrepreneurship. Their academic, business, research, consulting and teaching backgrounds combine to give them unique insight into the problems and opportunities of new ventures. The authors are entrepreneurs themselves. They have started a dozen businesses. They have known success and failure first hand, and they know what it takes to be successful. They closed one of their businesses after only a year. They grew a second business from $200,000 in sales in its first year to $2 million in sales in its second year. They sold it in the third year and moved on to new challenges. They started three nonprofit businesses and led them all to financial security. Today, they operate a thriving consulting practice and are sought after as speakers in entrepreneurship. For more than 20 years they have experienced the challenges of entrepreneurship and learned how the storm is weathered. They speak as doers and this book is founded on pragmatism.

Jim holds a PhD in Management Policy and Systems with related fields in Finance, Accounting and Economics. He was a Certified Management Accountant (inactive), a Certified Public Accountant (inactive), and a Certified Valuation Analyst (inactive). Jo Ann holds a PhD in Educational Psychology with minors in Social Dynamics, Statistics and Computer Systems. She held certificates as a Certified Data Processing Professional (inactive) and as a Certified Computer Professional (inactive). Jo Ann and Jim are prolific researchers. Together, they have published more than 200 articles and 12 books. They have made presentations to more than 200 groups throughout the United States and internationally and are recognized internationally as experts in entrepreneurship. They have published in such prestigious journals as the *Academy of Management Review*, the *Journal of Business Venturing*, the *International Journal of Management*, the *International Journal of Small Business*, the *Journal of Small Business Management*, *The American Journal of Small Business*, the *Journal of Business and Entrepreneurship,* the *Academy of Entrepreneurship Journal, The Entrepreneurial Executive,* and the *International Journal of Entrepreneurship.* Jim's depth and breadth of knowledge in strategy and planning is complemented by Jo Ann's skills in social dynamics, personality and behavior. They have consulted with more than 400 organizations, from not for profits, to microenterprises, to new ventures, to reorganizations, to recapitalizations, to major expansions and helped more than 100 people achieve their dreams of starting a business. They have seen and experienced entrepreneurship from the inside in both large and small ventures. They have experienced the thrill of success and the heartbreak of failure in their own firms. Their hard won secrets of entrepreneurship which will serve any entrepreneur are featured in the *Catching the American Dream* series, of which this book is a member.

Entrepreneurship is the foundation of the United States and the heart of the American Dream. Pioneers came to America in a search for economic opportunity, and they rapidly covered the world with Yankee trader ships. Today, the citizens of the world continue to recognize America as the land of opportunity and the multitude of immigrants attracted to the melting pot each year continue to seek out America in their own personal searches for economic self determination. There is no mystery as to why Americans, both native born and immigrant, dream of entrepreneurship. It is bred into the bones of this earth and it springs from the fountains of this land. Nothing is more sacred to Americans than the opportunity to dream a dream and the freedom to work to make that dream a reality.

That is what this series of books is about: the dream of entrepreneurship; how to turn that dream into a real, functioning, vibrant new venture, and how to grow that venture. The Drs. Carland have dreamed that dream, launched that venture, and helped hundreds of other dreamers and entrepreneurs along the way.

# Preface

Owning a successful business is the dream of millions of people. It can be one of the most rewarding experiences one can have, but far too many business start up attempts fail. We are convinced that failure is primarily a result of a lack of skills and planning. The fundamental objective of this book is to help potential entrepreneurs to develop the skills to become successful. The book has been written for individuals without experience or knowledge in business.

The study of entrepreneurial marketing should be fun as well as rewarding because it is, at heart, the study of dreams and making those dreams become realities.

We have designed the book around the key questions which a prospective entrepreneur must answer in order to start and manage a successful business. These include the personal issues facing a new business owner, discussed in Chapter 1, then progress through the practical issues of how to decide:

- ➔ what should go into a marketing plan,
- ➔ what to sell,
- ➔ where to locate, and,
- ➔ who your competitors will be,
- ➔ why people buy things,
- ➔ how you sell,
- ➔ how you set prices,
- ➔ what your costs are going to be,

From there, we proceed to explore the issues involved in:

- ➔ if you can breakeven,
- ➔ if your venture is feasible,
- ➔ how you promote and market your business
- ➔ if e-marketing is appropriate, and
- ➔ how to penetrate a new market.

Throughout the book, our concern has been to address the practical issues of successful business start up and operation. We have finessed the theory. We wanted a short, straight forward, simple discussion of the real life concerns which any prospective business owner must face. We use actual cases and examples to illustrate the issues throughout. We think that you will find it a no frills, clear, concise and readable exploration of one of the most important subjects in the world, and we hope that it will help you fulfill your dream.

Jim and JoAnn Carland

# TABLE OF CONTENTS

# CHAPTER ONE

## PERSONAL CONSIDERATIONS

### INTRODUCTION

Starting and managing your own successful business takes a lot of work and knowledge, but it is also one of the most rewarding experiences you can have. The rewards are not just financial. Most people find the personal satisfaction and sense of accomplishment even more valuable than money. But, in order to reap those benefits, your business must be successful. That takes planning. It takes understanding and insight. We will cover the basics of entrepreneurial marketing in this book: how you decide what you're going to sell; who your competition will be; why people buy things; how you sell things; how you price things; what your costs are going to be; how you promote your business; how to budget for your marketing efforts and, how you can make your business successful in the long term.

### THE DRIVE TO BE AN ENTREPRENEUR

Let's talk a minute about why people want to be entrepreneurs, why they want to go into business for themselves. Some entrepreneurs want to become wealthy. Sam Walton had an idea that a discount department store could be successful. He founded Wal-Mart in the early 1960s. It took years of hard work, but his idea was right. Walton eventually became the richest man in America and was worth billions at his death in 1992. Bill Gates started a company called Microsoft when he was 18 years old. That company specialized in system software for personal computers. Today, it is the largest software firm in the world. Bill Gates is a billionaire several times over and one of the wealthiest people in the world.

But, not everyone gets rich. In fact, most entrepreneurs **never** get rich. However, even those people who never get rich have rewards: the rewards of self satisfaction, of being your own boss. Most of all, the rewards are knowing that whatever success you have, it's a result of your own efforts. You are in charge of your own destiny. That's the reward.

What about you? Why do you want to start your own business? You must remember that starting and managing a business is a great deal of work. Business owners work longer hours than people who are employees in other firms, and most people do **not** get rich. In fact, some could make more money if they worked for someone else.

You hear about publicly owned companies every day on the business news. These are the businesses whose stock is traded on the New York Stock Exchange, the London Stock Exchange, the Tokyo Stock Exchange, the Hong Kong Stock Exchange, or one of the world's other stock exchanges. These companies only make up a small fraction of the businesses in the United States and in the world. Take the case of America. There are 20 million businesses in the United States and more than 19 million of them are businesses which are owned and operated by individuals. Most of these are very small, indeed. More than 90% of American firms have ten or fewer employees. Almost every business you come in contact with, is a business which is owned and operated by an entrepreneur. This can be confusing because sometimes the business may have the name of a large firm. Most of the McDonald's restaurants are franchises. That means that they are actually owned and operated by an entrepreneur. The owner pays a fee to McDonald's for using the name and to help pay for the national advertising.

Throughout the world, this model holds sway. The overwhelming majority of businesses in the world are owned and operated by entrepreneurs. Even when entrepreneurship was illegal in the old Soviet Union, the entrepreneurs operating outside the law made up the majority of businesses and provided goods and services which were in great demand throughout the nation. Not even governments cannot stop entrepreneurs; although governments can certainly make it more difficult to start and operate a business.

The point we want to make is that most of these millions upon millions of business owners are not really wealthy, although many of them do have a comfortable income. All of them do have the satisfaction of being their own boss, and of knowing that they are in charge of their own destiny. If that is the reward that you want, then starting your own business may be the best thing that you can do.

## SKILLS FOR SUCCESS

What does it take to start and manage a successful business? First, you must have some business skills. You must learn how a business works, what makes an idea feasible, and how a business sells its products or services. You must be able to evaluate an idea and a business, and you must be able to market and manage the operation. Then, you must plan. You must be willing to work and to work hard. Finally, you must be a self starter.

The majority of new business start ups do not succeed. Statistics kept by a variety of sources point to alarming failure rates. Dun and Bradstreet is a financial reporting company that keeps records on business failures. They report that 50% of all new American ventures fail during the first five years, with as few as two businesses out of ten surviving for 10 years. According to Dun and Bradstreet, the overwhelming majority of these failures are caused by poor management. In fact, they claim, lack of management experience accounts for 90% of all failures. On the plus side, not all of the failures result in bankruptcy. Many businesses are simply closed because their owners are tired, or bored, or don't have anyone to whom to leave the business, or can't find a buyer for the business. And, of course, failure in a business venture does not stop an individual from trying again. Many successful business owners have had business failures before finally becoming successful. Henry Ford failed twice before starting the Ford Motor Company, a company which changed the world and put America on wheels. We have been there ourselves, having to close more than one business which we started, but we learned a great deal from those experiences and we did not let it discourage us.

The point we want to make is that good planning could prevent most of the business failures. That's why we have such a heavy emphasis on planning in this book. We have had many clients over the years who have experienced problems in starting and managing their businesses and we have experienced such problems ourselves. Problems inevitably result from a failure to follow good planning practices. With proper planning, an idea which is not feasible can be adjusted to make it feasible. We can change the scale of the business, its location, how it will do business, any one of a myriad of aspects which can change a potential failure into a potential success. That's why we wrote this book and that is what we will focus on: making sure that your business will be a success.

The last thing we mentioned is the willingness to work. Many surveys have been done over the years and all of them indicate that entrepreneurs work much longer hours than most people think. In one poll conducted for the *Wall Street Journal*, the results showed that 24% of business owners worked 70 or more hours per week. In fact, only 19% of them worked *less than* 50 hours per week. Almost no one worked a 40 hour week. These were managers of existing businesses. During the start up phase of a business venture, you should expect to work much harder, and much longer hours than will be required later. It may not be necessary to be a workaholic to be successful in a business venture, but it helps.

Finally, you must remember that in a new business venture, there is no one to push, pull or persuade the boss. The owner must be a self starter and self motivator. Being the boss means that there is no one to tell you when to go to work, or what to do after you get there. There is no one to encourage you when you feel depressed or discouraged. You will never be able to manage other people if you cannot manage yourself. The best way to do that is to plan. Planning serves the purpose of a tool to evaluate and control your business and it also serves as a tool to keep yourself going in the right direction.

## FINANCIAL REQUIREMENTS

The short answer is yes. It takes money to start a business. Statistics show that the primary source of money used to start businesses is personal savings and loans from family members. Many people have the misconception that all you need to do is take your idea to a bank and borrow the money. It doesn't work that way. No bank will be willing to risk a great deal of money in a business which is just getting started, especially if the owner is inexperienced. You can get some capital from banks, but generally, you must have a large part of the money you will need before you can borrow any more. Keep in mind a general rule of thumb: no one is going to be willing to risk more money in a new venture than the owner is risking.

That does not necessarily mean that you must have half of the money needed to start the business. It means that your risk must be as great as any investor or any lender. Investors and lenders believe that if you have little money invested in a venture, you may be inclined to walk away if things get tough. If you have everything tied up in the business, you are more likely to stay and work through problems. In general that translates into a requirement for you to invest a really significant amount in the business and to assume a level of risk which demonstrates your confidence in the venture and in yourself.

## THE ROLE OF KNOWLEDGE

The starting point for a prospective entrepreneur is knowledge. We will begin by seeking answers to the questions of what to sell, where to locate and who your competitors will be. Then we will explore why people buy things, how you sell and how you set prices. At that point we will turn to the key issues of what your costs are going to be and, the most important question of all, can your idea for a business venture be successful.

We will help you develop the skills necessary to promote and market your business. Knowledge is required to launch and manage a thriving business and we will focus on the practical, down to earth skills which you need. We begin with what you are going to sell.

## REVIEW

People go into business for themselves for different reasons and at different times in their lives, but the primary reason most people give when asked is that they want to be their own boss. This process if you want to be successful requires planning, not serendipity. Too many small businesses fail every year because they did not plan well before startup and did not continue to plan during operations.

Commitment is required. Hard work is mandated. Some capital is required, but wise planning is the key to success. Knowledge, confidence and business skills can make you successful. Just plan and you can fulfill your dreams!

## QUESTIONS, EXERCISES AND CASES

### Questions

1. What is the principal cause of failure in small business?

2. Discuss the failure statistics cited and state how one might learn from these statistics.

3. Why do you suppose that being a workaholic is important?

4. Why is capital an important requirement for start up in the small business environment?

5. Discuss the several causes of business failures.

6. Do you know of such a failure based upon your personal knowledge? Explain.

7. What can one do to reduce the risk of failure in a small business?

### Exercise

1, Check on the SBA website and see what is listed as causes of business failure.

2. Are there businesses in your town which have gone out of buisness. Can you determine why?

### Case

Joan McCoy was a young lady who was a very good cook. She loved making gourmet meals for friends and neighbors. Many times she would be asked to make dainties for showers and weddings and felt quite good about what she was doing. Her husband, while he wanted to encourage his wife's enjoyment, felt that when she counted her time and the massive storehouse of ingredients required by her hobby she was getting very little in return for her effort.

Jim McCoy worked as an accountant in a large textile plant and was concerned about his job. The textile industry was facing enormous cutbacks and even though he had been with the firm since graduation, he knew that he would be the first to go in a cutback in his department. Because of his job concerns, Jim was also upset about the personal expenditures at home. Joan was having a ball cooking for others and eating up the praise which came her way at each and every function where her wares were displayed and tasted. When the McCoys were financially secure, there was no problem, but now with Jim's job at risk, the extra expenses incurred by Joan were straining their already tenuous relationship.

One evening in an effort to return their relationship to an even keel, Jim and Joan sat down and discussed frankly what was happening to their marriage; to their lives and what could be done to improve the situation. Jim was worried about losing his job even though he had not been happy there for a number of years. His job represented stability and was non threatening. Joan wanted to work but her greatest asset seemed to be in feeding others. A friend, who was aware of the strain Joan and Jim were under, and who happened to be a local businessman suggested that the two open a bakery or sandwich shop. The McCoys were immediately interested. Working together in a business of their own might be the perfect solution.

After discussing what was necessary to begin with their friend, they decided to invest their savings in the start up of a bakery. Jim because of his accounting background and a business major in college knew some of the aspects of management and marketing and therefore would handle the managerial functions of the bakery and Joan would take care of producing the goods. If the business grew, they could hire some people to help out in the cooking area. The excitement of working together and knowing that success depended on themselves alone filled all their time together. The McCoys were ready to go. They began to plan the opening of their business.

1. What aspects of the case make it reasonable to assume that if they plan wisely, the McCoys might make a success of their bakery?

2. What obstacles might they need to overcome to insure their successful venture?

3. If you were the McCoys would you engage in this new venture? Why or why not?

4. List other alternatives to actually going into business which the McCoys might pursue initially if capital were a problem.

5. How might the McCoys raise the capital for their venture?

# CHAPTER TWO

## ENTREPRENEURIAL MARKETING

### INTRODUCTION

Here we will focus on an overview of *Entrepreneurial Marketing*, which is the process of establishing the existence of a viable market for a product or service and planning for the successful launch of a venture which provides those products and/or services. We will explore the steps one should take to establish the existence of a market for a product or service and the initial marketing plan. Be assured that we will explore all of the various steps in great depth in later units. Here, we want to provide an outline which will help to bind the various aspects together in your mind as we present them in later units. In our minds, the key to *Entrepreneurial Marketing*, like to key to anything else, is *Planning*. Consequently, we will present the topics in the form of a *Marketing Plan.*

One word of warning is valid at this point. *Your own judgement as to the value of a product or service is not necessarily valid.* Just because you would be willing to buy an item or service is no guarantee that there are sufficient numbers of people in your market area to make a business based on that item successful. Market research is required to answer that question. Further, even if there is sufficient demand for a particular item in a particular area, it will not automatically be successful. The manner in which the item is offered for sale will be a major factor in determining its success. You can't just open a store. You have to *sell* your goods and services.

### THE NEED FOR PLANNING

As a first step, the prospective entrepreneur owner should determine why he or she wishes to start a business and what the desired outcome of the venture should be. The prospective owner should evaluate his or her skills, strengths and weaknesses and determine what the price of the venture will be in terms of personal time, effort and dedication. We talked about this in the introductory unit, so now, we will turn to marketing. The marketing portion of the business plan is reproduced in Table 1. (The broader Business Plan is the subject of other units, and we concentrate here solely on Entrepreneurial Marketing.) The table indicates that the evaluation of the product or service and the evaluation of the market area are separate steps. We show it that way to emphasize the importance of the evaluation of both the offerings and the area in which the offerings are to be sold. In practice, however, the two aspects are generally evaluated at the same time.

**Table 1: The Entrepreneurial Marketing Plan**

| | | |
|---|---|---|
| II. | Choose a Product or Service | |
| | 1. | Evaluate the marketability of the product/service |
| | 2. | Determine feasibility of product/service |
| III. | Select Market Area | |
| | 1. | Evaluate market area |
| | 2. | Determine feasibility of market area |
| | 3. | Evaluate the competition |

The first step in the marketing plan is the selection of the product or service which is to be sold. As we will discuss in later units, many people choose a product based upon situations or past experience. Others discover a product or service which they think no one is addressing and for which they believe a large market exists. Both approaches have value. Experience with the product or service which you intend to sell helps you to understand what is required to produce the items and what is required to sell them.

## DEVELOPING A MARKETING PLAN

We will explore in depth the "who, what, when, where, how and why" of the buying decision. These are critical issues which we will want you to master. Consider how important it is to identify *who* the consumers of the product or service are; *what* it is that they are really purchasing; *when* the purchase transactions take place for our product or service; *where* the sale actually occurs; *how* the sales transaction is handled; and, *why* a prospective customer would wish to buy our product or service. Further, we will explored the three basic approaches to marketing: push marketing, pull marketing and piggyback marketing strategies. In *push* strategies the focus is on encouraging the intermediary supplier rather than the ultimate consumer to stock our goods; in *pull* marketing the focus is on persuading the ultimate consumer that he or she desires our products or services for some specific reason; and, in *piggyback* strategies we allow a competitor to create and attract a market which we will try to take away on the basis of price or some other factor. In addition, we will discuss the techniques of marketing research and we will stress the importance of the business image and the need for consistency. We will examine the concept of a distinctive competency which will set our business apart from its competitors: a factor which our customers will think of when they think about our business. Taking all of these factors into consideration, Entrepreneurial Marketing requires us to establish a plan for the penetration of our target market, in our target market area. Table 2 present the steps involved in that plan in outline format.

Steps one through five of the plan are iterative. That means that the venture should not be initiated nor the entrepreneurial marketing plan finalized until products and/or services and the market area are deemed to be viable based upon the market research.

**Table 2: The Entrepreneurial Marketing Plan**

1. Select products or services to be offered;
2. Select the area in which the business is to be located;
3. Conduct market research;
4. Examine products or services and area for viability;
5. Change products, services or areas as necessary;
6. Select alternative sites for the business;
7. Establish pricing strategies and policies;
8. Establish promotional strategies;
9. Establish the budget for start-up marketing;
10. Determine the image to be portrayed;
11. Make the final site selection;
12. Establish the marketing plan.

## PRODUCT AND SERVICE SELECTION

Most people select a product or service with which they have experience or for which they believe an untapped demand exists. The market research is made simpler in the former instance, but is still required. In the latter instance potential difficulties exist resulting from lack of familiarity with the items which are to be offered for sale. It is always better to have experience with an item when possible. If not possible, then the acquisition of people with appropriate experience should be a high priority. Starting off in a new venture with a product or service with which you have no experience and without knowledge in the firm from other sources makes the venture more risky and success more difficult to obtain. If you intend to start such a venture, be especially sure that the market research has been well and thoroughly done!

Stories abound about fortunes made by the inventor of a new product. The truth is that many inventors and innovators are *not* successful. We just don't hear about the failures. If your product or service is a new one for which a market does not really exist, then be forewarned that success in a business based on that item will not be easily achieved. The real success stories for new items frequently involve a venture which has been well funded and in which talented people in a variety of areas have been recruited. The days of a single inventor being able to start a million dollar business on a shoe string are gone forever: if they ever existed!

## AREA SELECTION

The ***market area*** is that geographic territory from which you can expect sales to come and is a part of the site selection process. Most people starting a new venture do not pay enough attention to the issue of area selection. All too often the area chosen is simply the one in which the originator lives at the time. The area chosen will have a profound impact on the ultimate success of the company. As the market research should show, the size and viability of demand for the offerings of a new business vary by geographic area.

There are a host of publications available which can provide insight into the area selection process. The Census Bureau publishes materials which contain not only the basic demographic data about every area in the country but also include a host of business factors as well. The Small Business Administration also produces publications designed to help in area and site selection. In fact, all of the states have a business development office whose function is to provide information to prospective business start-ups within the state. These offices collect business and demographic data which can be of assistance not only in choosing a state in which to locate, but a region within that state as well. Most of this information is available free or at a small charge. Contact your local SBA office or the SBA office or Census Bureau in Washington, DC, or the office of business development in each of the respective state capitals. Local chambers of commerce frequently collect data of interest to small businesses and are always happy to assist a prospective new business. One of the publications available from the SBA is a compilation of statistics which show the number of people which are needed in an area to support a particular kind of business. Combine that information with a population count from the Census Bureau and you will have a much better idea of the potential viability of an area. In most nations of the world, counterparts to all of these agencies and bureaus exist. Finding them and exploiting them is just an exercise in creativity.

In order to make maximum use of data about an area, you need to know the characteristics of your target market. We will dive into this subject in later units, but for now consider that ***target markets*** are classified according to age, sex, income, occupation, family status, etc. ***Demographics*** are more than population counts. Census data and data available from state and local sources will also include income and other factors. That means that a firm understanding of target market will make the utilization of demographic data more effective.

A more particular classification of your target market is through ***psychographics***. These are characteristics of your target market which are based on the desires, interests and preferences of the people in the market. Consider that you are interested in running a music store, selling cds, tapes, videos, etc. for music fans and buffs. You can try to stock everything, but you will quickly find that you will need a really large store and a really large inventory. This will drive your operational costs up, and make your break even point higher. On the other hand, you can decide to specialize in one or two types of music. This will mean that you are appealing to a subset of the target market which embodies the psychographic desire for the types of music you choose. Each type of music embodies a different psychographic, from country music, to rock music, to hip hop, etc.

Psychographics are involved in every aspect of market specialization and may be far more critical than demographics. Consider a store which features "vintage clothing." If you are not familiar with that concept, you may not be aware that a large number of stores sell what many people would consider to be old, used clothing. The trick is that the clothing is gleaned from yard sales, estate sales, and an increasing number of suppliers who are searching for and finding old clothing which is wearable and which embodies an aspect of historic fashion. This can be anything from frock coats, to hoop dresses, to bell bottom trousers, to zoot suits, etc. The success of these stores revolves around finding these sartorial treasures from the past, and presenting them to the carefully selected psychographic market of vintage clothing wearers.

Psychographics go far beyond collectors and a modern embodiment of the power of market sector identification appears in the "green movement." A huge number of people today are interested in environmental protection and in natural products and in services which produce a small and limited impact on the planet. These people display a psychographic nature which allows a business to target their interests and desires through careful product and service selection, and highly targeted advertising and marketing.

## AREA SELECTION AND COMPETITION

One of the prime factors involved in area selection is the existence of direct competitors. A ***direct competitor*** is one with which you will be competing *head to head*; one who carries the same basic items or provides the same basic services as you will. ***Indirect competitors***, on the other hand, will offer competition for some items which you carry, but not all, or will offer competition for the dollars which your customers can spend. An example of the latter situation is the competition offered to a movie theater by an arcade. Both offer entertainment and are therefore competitors for the entertainment dollars of the market area, but they are not direct competitors because they offer different kinds of entertainment.

Contrary to the usual first impression, it is easier to start a business in an area which has direct competition than in one which does not. Piggyback marketing strategies are possible in such areas, whereas they are not in areas without direct competitors. To be successful in an area in which direct competitors exist, you need only do a better job than the established firms. To be successful in an area in which no direct competitors exist, you must create a market. That may be simple in the case of a product or service which a community has long desired, such as a theater in a small town which prevents people from driving to the city. On the other hand it may be quite difficult. The establishment of a microcomputer retail store in that same small town could be a risky venture!

## MARKET RESEARCH

The kind of business you intend to start has an effect on the area required. Access to the target market and a market of sufficient size are the primary criteria. For a manufacturing business, area requirements could include a ready supply of labor and access to transportation networks. For a construction company, area requirements might be major population growth which would drive new home construction. For a wholesaler, access to manufacturers or jobbers, and to retail customers could be the primary consideration. For other firms, the regulatory environment could be a key. One client of ours selected the Atlanta, Georgia area to start a local delivery trucking company. The city required trucks delivering within the city limits to have a permit, and the city was extremely reluctant to issue new permits. That meant that established firms held a strong competitive position. Our client located a small trucking company whose owner wished to retire, bought the firm to obtain access to the delivery permit, and established a highly successful operation.

In all cases the area to be considered must be researched to determine its suitability for the venture. We mentioned the use of Census Bureau, SBA, state business development offices and local chambers of commerce, and their international equivalents, as sources of information about an area. Don't overlook the possibility of personal research. In a later unit, we will tell you the story of two young people who decided to open a pizza restaurant in a college town which already had 18 pizzerias. They conducted a survey of the established competition by personally visiting every pizza restaurant in town. They looked the place over, bought dinner, watched the customers, evaluated the service, hours, location and menu of every competitor. This research was a major factor in their ability to open a successful restaurant. As a matter of fact, they continue to do this on a regular basis today! There is no substitute for personal investigation.

The process of market research to determine area suitability starts with an understanding of the venture which you will begin and the characteristics of the target market which you wish to tap. Once that has been determined, you know what kinds of information about an area you require. That makes your research more effective and improves your ability to interpret all types of data, including information from published sources.

Don't overlook general information about an area. It is easy to get lost in demographic and psychographic detail and overlook pertinent information such as number and stability of employers, economic conditions and prospects for future growth. Strong insight into the viability of an area can be obtained by investigation through the local employment security commission. Not only can this agency help you find prospective employees, it can give you information about unemployment levels, skill levels of the work force, nature and number of employers in the area, and a host of other factors.

The local zoning board can also be a goldmine of information. Not only will it be able to show you where various types of industry can be located, it can show you concentrations of potential competitors. The zoning board can also give you insight into locations which may be suitable for your business. That can avoid problems like those of one entrepreneur who bought land and built a grocery store based on traffic count data and accessibility. After construction was under way, he learned that the city limits were about 1,000 feet short of his location which meant that he must operate under county laws. The county prohibited the sale of beer and wine! This was a major setback because the other grocery stores in town could sell beer and wine giving them a competitive edge.

Just keeping your mind open and thinking about what might occur in the future is an important characteristic. For example, if you are pursuing a piggyback strategy in which you intend to locate close to competitors to benefit from their draws, be sure that those competitors are strong. One entrepreneur that we know of established an inexpensive motel across the street from a Holiday Inn in an attempt to siphon off business based on price competition. Little did he know that the HI was not doing all that well. Less than a year later, the Holiday Inn was sold to a discount hotel chain which changed its name and reduced its rates, wiping out his price advantage! This can happen even in a mall. Malls traditionally have a high turnover of stores, and the choice of a location based upon the surrounding stores could easily lose its luster as stores fail and are replaced by other vendors.

## MARKET VIABILITY

To assess the viability of a new venture, we must evaluate the market for a product or service. We must conduct market research and compare the market information with the financial needs for the new venture. In simple terms, ***market viability*** means the ease with which a new company can sell enough to make a profit in a specific area and location. In essence, the assessment of viability is the judgment that a sufficient market demand exists in the area for the offerings of a business to make that business successful. In the case of a business whose market area is not constrained by its location, such as an Internet based business, the viability of an area will be based on other success factors. These might include access to shipping, warehousing or suppliers, or they could be such factors as regulatory environment, labor pool and conditions, etc.

Viability is often a subjective evaluation. That means that it cannot be computed mathematically, but is a matter of judgment. Breakeven analysis, which we will teach you, can tell you how much you have to sell, but the determination as to whether that number can be achieved remains a judgement call. Market research can help to make that judgement stronger. For example, if you know that a population base of a certain level is required to support your business, it is easy to determine whether such a population base exists in a given area and location. To do that you must accumulate the information.

The best approach to market research is to make a list of the factors which will be important in making your business successful. Be specific and make the list as complete as you possibly can. Then make a list of potential areas for location. You can make the initial list based on areas in which you would like to live. Research each of the success factors for each of the areas. Assess the market viability and eliminate areas. Once a viable area has been found, repeat the process with locations within the area. Remember that if an area is not deemed to be viable, then a new area or new products or services should be selected and the process of market research and evaluation repeated. Until you feel comfortable with the probability of success in an area with a particular business configuration, you should not proceed with the business venture. You have not established its feasibility until you have determined that you can produce a profit in the selected market area, with the selected target market!

## ALTERNATIVE SITE SELECTION

The selection of the actual location of a business within the market area has cost/benefit tradeoffs. That means that some sites will cost more, but may be more valuable from the perspective of the amount of business which can be expected to occur at that site. The business site is more important for some types of businesses than it is for others. If the business is one in which customers will be expected to come to the business location, then the site is obviously more important than it would be if sales people were to be used who call on customers at other locations. It is very difficult to make the evaluation as to a particular site, especially when there are limited funds as is usually the case in a new venture. Traffic patterns, both automobile and pedestrian, as well as public transport access, ease of access, visibility, makeup of the surrounding area and a host of other factors play a role in the relative worth of a business site. A good starting point is to look for where the competition is located. Site selection can be piggybacked just like marketing strategies. Footwork should also be used. Get out and look at alternatives sites. Draw up a list of the sites which you are considering and record their good points and their bad points. In other words, use the same procedure we outlined above: list desirable factors, list alternative locations, research the factors for each location. Remember that a more expensive location should not be automatically eliminated. Consider as many alternatives as you can before making a final selection. The site you finally select is going to be with you for a while. Make sure it is the right one for your business.

One final point needs to be made about site selection. In later units we will stress the importance of the image which you wish to portray to your customers. The site which you finally select is a major part of that image. If you are opening a professional services business, then a prestigious address may be required to support such an image. If you are opening a discount retail business, an address in a shopping mall could be a disadvantage because it carries with it the image of expensive stores. The final decision about the location which you will acquire cannot be made until you have finalized the image for your business.

## FINAL SITE SELECTION

As we mentioned earlier, the final site selection should include consideration of the image as well as the cost/benefit tradeoffs which you should have analyzed for each of the alternative sites. If none of the sites seem to fit, then more should be sought until you are well pleased with the result. It is an expensive process to relocate a business. Lease terms frequently make it impossible during the first several years.

Be sure to allow for change or growth in your business in the site selection as well. Try to visualize what the business will be like in a year or two if it is successful. One liquor store with which we worked had selected a fine site in a shopping center, but located in an inner space thereby eliminating drive-up service options. When the business grew and customers began to desire drive-up service, the business was forced to relocate. The landlord required a substantial sum for early release from a five year lease. That penalty could have been avoided, because at the time of the original lease, a corner location was available for a small additional rental. Our client had tried to save a few dollars and ended up spending much more. The moral of the story is, don't think about minimum needs, think about what you really need, and might really grow into, when you are trying to make the site selection.

## PRICING AND PROMOTIONAL STRATEGIES

How much is a product or service worth? There is no answer to this question. As we will discuss in later units, we can't even be sure we know what it is that a customer is buying when they purchase goods and services from us. In the pizza example that we mentioned, our young couple's customers appeared to be buying entertainment rather than pizza, because the restaurant that they built was one in which they encouraged a large number of college students to hang out, and they made the restaurant the place to go. Obviously, this would not have happened if the customers felt that prices were too high. On the other hand, mink coats are not sold in department stores. People who purchase such items expect a level of service from the sales staff which is inconsistent with department stores. Furthermore, they don't expect to find a discount mink coat. Clearly, a furrier can have a sale on furs and can have success with that sale, but the items are sold differently and price is less of a factor than with many other goods.

Cost is really not an important consideration in pricing, contrary to popular opinion. Prices can be perceived by customers as low even when mark ups are quite high. Consider the case of expensive jewelry. Mark ups of 300% are common, although customers may still perceive these as low. On the other hand, grocery store mark ups tend to be extremely low on staple goods, 10% to 15%, but customers still make price comparisons and may perceive these prices as high. As you can see, it is customer *perceptions* which make prices high or low, not costs!

How many times have you heard people say that prices must be high enough to at least cover costs? We will learn that there are many different types of costs. It is true that no business can sell for less than variable costs over the long term and be successful, but as long as variable costs are covered, fixed costs can be absorbed by volume sales. This may not even be as static as it sounds. When Texas Instruments was a young, entrepreneurial venture, it got into the calculator business. Competition was quite heavy. TI grossly undercut the prices of all of its competitors, but they responded by cutting their prices as well. TI recognized that its labor force was becoming more proficient at manufacturing calculators, remarkably so, and decided to capitalize on that learning curve. They actually priced calculators below their own costs in anticipation that those costs would drop as the volume of sales went up and labor continued to improve its efficiency. The strategy worked; competitors did not feel able to match the extremely low prices; volume did grow and efficiency grew with it; TI was able to establish a major market share in calculators and become profitable as manufacturing costs dropped.

In a more recent example, Amazon.com dropped the prices on its e-book reader to below its own costs. It expected to gain a larger market share of the e-book market and to make up for its losses with future sales of e-books to its larger e-book reader base. The strategy worked, and Amazon gained a march on its competitors. Time will tell whether the advantage is long lived!

None of that helps in establishing initial prices or promotional strategies for a new venture. Then how does one go about it? The first step is to assess the competition. There are three basic pricing strategies: ***pricing at the market***, ***pricing below the market***, or, ***pricing above the market***. ***Pricing below the market*** implies that a major aspect of your business will be price competition. That is, you will be attempting to win business based on having a lower price. ***Pricing above the market*** implies that you will be striving to win business based on quality, image, location, service, or other factors. ***Pricing at the market*** implies that you will be striving to remove price considerations from the purchase decision. In other words, you will not want price to be a factor in the customers' purchase decision.

Each of the approaches has advantages and disadvantages. However, pricing below the market can be dangerous for a new venture because established competitors can retaliate by lowering their prices as well in an attempt to force out the new company before it has a chance to get established. If the start-up can weather such a storm as Texas Instruments did, then this could be a viable strategy. But, if a venture is weak financially, as most are, and cannot afford a battle with established competitors, pricing below the market can be risky.

Pricing above the market also carries significant risk. If the firm is unable to establish in the minds of its customers a belief that the higher price is justified by quality or other factors, the business may not be able to establish itself. Nevertheless, during the early months of a new venture, customers tend to be more cognizant of prices because they have not yet established an image of the business in their minds. Furthermore, all of the customers have been purchasing from other firms and are therefore aware of price discrepancies. An established business is more likely to be able to price slightly above the market without its clientele realizing that fact than is a new venture.

As you can see from the foregoing, the least risky pricing strategy is to price at the market. This infers that competition will be based on other features than price. Be aware that when we talk about market price there are fluctuations which result from image differences. In other words, there are multiple prices for a product or service in the market place. For example, men's suits have an established price range in department stores. They have another established price range in discount stores. Tax preparation services have an established price in CPA firms. They have another established price in accounting firms and still another in tax preparation chain stores.

When you set out to establish the market price for your goods or services, you must be sure to examine competitors with the same approach or image as that which you will be pursuing. Of course, that implies that the image of the business will be established before its pricing policies.

That is the case with much of the marketing effort because consistency of price, location, hours, service, promotion, etc., can only be obtained if each is consistent with the image of the business.

There is one other point about pricing which must be made. If you will carry multiple products or services, all must be priced consistently. You cannot be lower than the market in some areas and higher in others because your customers will be confused by the differences and will not be able to formulate an image of your business in their minds. This confusion may not be voiced, but it will exist and it will cause many customers to feel uncomfortable with your business.

Promotion strategies cannot be set until pricing strategies have been established, both of which must follow the image of the business. ***Promotion*** is more than advertising. Non-advertising aspects of promotion include signs, layout, point of sale promotional pieces, letters, notes or cards to be mailed to customers periodically, special events and sales, to name a few. Every aspect of your business which is or which can be seen by customers is an aspect of promotion. It is no accident that sales people in multiple industries send their customers birthday cards; retailers send customers private announcements of sales; people in services businesses send newsletters, etc. All of these efforts are oriented at obtaining and maintaining visibility in the eyes of the customer. You want your present and prospective customers to think of your business often and in a positive light. When they are ready to buy, you don't want them to shop! You want them to call you!

Effective promotion requires constant planning. Before the venture is established, you should consider various approaches to obtaining visibility, ensure that they are consistent with the image you want to portray, and establish a time table for their execution. One locally owned furniture store with which we are familiar has a sale every single month. Each sale has a different name and each promises huge discounts off the manufacturer's retail price. The truth is that the store is actually a discount furniture store and the prices offered are those the store would charge anyway. Nevertheless, the sales do work! The store sells the vast majority of each month's volume in the week long sale. Furthermore, the constant exposure from sales promotions makes the store's name a household word.

## MARKETING BUDGET

People frequently think of the start-up capital requirements for a new venture strictly in terms of what it will cost to acquire any initial inventory, equipment, supplies, etc., and what will be required to cover initial operating expenses for some period of time. That is not adequate. The start-up budget must include monies for the start-up marketing and the operating expenses must include an allowance for ongoing marketing expenditures as well. Obviously funds will be limited, but inventory, equipment, supplies, leasehold improvements, and the like will not be valuable to a company which has no customers. Marketing is expensive, but it is also vital.

Discussions with advertising agencies can be valuable. Such firms are expensive, which may be why few small business start-ups use them, but you should at least investigate the possibility of employing an agency and discussing what kinds of start-up advertising campaigns they suggest. Talk to more than one agency and discuss agencies with other business owners, with bankers, with the chamber of commerce and others. The selection of a good agency could be a valuable step in the marketing plan. If you decide not to go with an advertising agency, let that decision be the result of conscious thought: not the result of a failure to consider the alternative.

If you decide to handle your own marketing, then talk to the various media representatives in the area and get circulation or coverage data as well as prices. Don't overlook outdoor advertising or direct mail. You should explore the cost of mailing lists and printing costs for brochures. The Chamber of Commerce can give you ideas about sources of mailing lists as can other businesses, bankers, state and federal assistance offices, etc., and the Internet is an absolute goldmine of information. In addition, most larger communities have directories available which list the names and addresses of the population. The Chamber can help you with that as well.

The start-up marketing budget is really the result of planning the initial advertising and estimating its cost. The start-up operating budget for a new venture should generally incorporate some *slack* in case you have overlooked or underestimated some expenses. This is also a good idea for the marketing budget. Once you have estimated the requirements, add some more in case you have overlooked something, or in case a second advertising push is required to get the business rolling.

## THE BUSINESS IMAGE

As we have mentioned repeatedly, nothing is more important to the success of a business venture than the image which it will portray to its customers. You should consider carefully how you wish your customers to perceive your business and how your business will be distinct from its direct and indirect competition. Whatever image you decide upon, you must be consistent with everything else, especially, the advertising. In large measure, the advertising approach which you take initially in a new venture will set the tone for the image which the business will have in the minds of its customers.

## THE MARKETING PLAN

The start-up marketing plan includes much more than the initial advertising. The plan should address the opening date, the initial marketing budget, start-up advertising and its media, and beginning promotional plans. The purpose of the plan is to gain rapid recognition among the target market and to persuade potential customers to examine the offerings. Frequently, an advertising campaign will be accompanied by sales prices, contests or prizes or other attention gainers. The plan should allow for a time table for the various aspects of the start-up of the venture. All aspects of the start-up must be coordinated. Staffing concerns are not the least of these. One restaurant with which we are familiar, held its grand opening after much start-up advertising and promotional coupons, but neglected to train the temporary waiters and waitresses who were hired to handle the expected opening night crowds. The expected crowds did appear, but the staff confused the orders, forgot to replenish the salad bar, and became exasperated and distraught. Many of the customers left, vowing never to return. Everything had been done perfectly and the advertising and promotions had attracted tremendous attention. One small detail, the training of six temporary staff members, turned the grand opening into a catastrophe from which the business may never recover.

## GENERALIZING THE MARKETING PLAN

The process which we have described in this unit for developing a start-up marketing plan applys to any type of venture. Service businesses tend to overlook some aspects of the process because theirs is a venture which depends upon people rather than things. This is a mistake. It may be true for a particular type of business that some aspects of the start-up are less important than others. For example, site location may be less important to a firm which never expects customers to come to its offices. This does not mean that any of the steps are unimportant or that any should be skipped. Only by systematically proceeding through the process can the pitfalls of starting a business be minimized. Just as in meeting people, first impressions are hard to change, the first impressions which customers develop of a new business are hard to overcome. The only way to ensure that those impressions are positive is to plan.

## REVIEW

The first step in starting a new business is selecting the product or service to be sold. The product or service can be chosen based upon experience or to fulfill a recognized niche in the marketplace. In either case, strategies must be designed to attract public attention.

The steps in the marketing plan are outlined in Table 2. The steps in the plan are generalizable to service and other types of businesses as well as the traditional retailer. Some steps will be more important for a specific business than will be others. Nevertheless, none of the steps can be omitted or else the prospective business owners risks initial mistakes which can be costly and difficult to correct in the future.

Now, it's time to dive into the details of the entrepreneurial marketing plan. The first step, if you remember, is choosing your product or service, and that is the subject of the next chapter.

# QUESTIONS, EXERCISES AND CASES

## Questions

1. Why is your own personal judgement about the marketability of an item invalid?

2. Discuss and/or review the who, what, when, where and how of the marketing process.

3. Name and describe the three approaches to marketing.

4. How does market research affect the success of a new product/service in its selection?

5. What is market area and why is its selection important?

6. What is the difference between direct and indirect competition?

7. Why is your choice of products/services and market area iterative?

8. What are some of the considerations in determining site selection for your business?

9. Why is a marketing budget important and what areas should you examine in determining your marketing alternatives?

10. List and explain the components of the marketing plan.

## Exercise

1. Take a look in your neighborhood. Observe several businesses to see if they have a marketing plan which is observable. If they advertise, rate the methods used. In conjunction with deciding about marketing plans, evaluate the image, location and product/service. Do these attributes indicate planning or happenstance?

2. Are any new businesses starting up in your town? What types of activities can you see that might indicate a marketing strategy? Does it appear that they have a marketing plan? Do you think that what they are doing will work? What would you do?

**Case**

Mark Davis was a conscientious young man who was determined to be successful. He wanted to set up a really neat bar in the university town which he had adopted. He had gone to school there and was finishing up his MBA. This was where he wanted to stay. After having spent nearly six years in this town as a student, he knew that there were few places that students could really go and have fun. The town was progressive in the sense that the sale of beer/wine/liquor was possible, but the only places in town where one could go and drink on the premises would be classified as "joints". Mark had visited some of these places with some friends and found them to be a bit rough. The customers were serious drinkers and didn't much cater to the younger crowd who wanted music and fun.

Mark decided to approach this decision to open a pub realistically. He wanted to create an atmosphere where students could meet or date and dance, listen to music and relax, but he wanted to be successful most of all. He visited the nearest Small Business Development Center and asked for their advice about starting his business. He needed to make a loan, acquire a site, hire some people, and do some marketing. He worked with the consultants assigned to him and everything was looking good. His case worker told him that his success would depend upon how well his initial marketing campaign was carried out and whether he could get some capital. So Mark began to do some planning.

1. What kind of site do you think Mark should find?

2. What external or legal constraints might Mark have in starting a bar?

3. What kinds of planning should Mark do to see if the bar itself is a viable alternative?

4. Who would be Mark's competition?

5. How would Mark build an image for his bar which would accommodate drinks, snacks and dancing which would be more pleasing to him?

6. What would probably be his target market?

7. Prepare an initial marketing plan for Mark's business.

8. Obtain cost estimates for the locations which you consider appropriate for such a business and estimate the cost for the promotion and advertising plans that you have prepared for the business.

# CHAPTER THREE

## SELECTING PRODUCTS AND SERVICES

### INTRODUCTION

Now that you've decided you want to be your own boss, what are you planning to sell? It can be a product or a service, but in either case, you *will* have to sell it. Have you ever heard that famous quote from Ralph Waldo Emerson? It comes from a lecture he gave in 1871 and it goes like this:

> *If a man can write a better book, preach a better sermon, or make a better mouse trap than his neighbor, though he builds his house in the woods, the world will make a beaten path to his door.*

It sounds beautiful doesn't it? The only problem is that it's just not true. The truth is that Mr. Emerson was a bit naive. He failed to take the time factor into consideration. Your product or service may be better than anybody else's, but if you don't market it, by the time the world discovers what you have and beats a path to your door, you will be out of business. There is another old adage which is much closer to the truth: *'nothing happens until somebody sells something.'*

### CHOOSING A PRODUCT

People tend to choose a product or service because they think they know something about it or because they think there is a market for it, or both. Product simply means the tangible items which you offer for sale. There may be a whole range of items, like in a hardware store, but we call the group of items hardware and we say this is your product. It's simply a way to classify what you're selling. If the things you are selling are not tangible, we say you are selling a service. Again, there may be a whole range of things you are selling, like a carpentry shop, but we call the group of services carpentry and we say this is your service.

The actual mix of products or services which you sell is important, of course, because it can distinguish your business from others like it. For example, if you knew something about baking and thought you had some skill in that area, you might decide to open a bakery. The type of baked goods which you stock in your store will make up your product mix. You might decide to specialize in breads while other bakeries specialize in cakes and donuts. That would distinguish you from your competition. If you're right in guessing that there is a market for bread in your market area, you will be successful.

When we talk about this market, we really mean the group of people who want what you're selling. This is also called demand. The people who want your product or service, who demand your product or service, are called the market. The area which your business can serve is called the market area. Usually this means the town or the city or the county. It's where the people who will be your customers live. If there are a large number of people in the market area who will buy what you're selling, we say the market is large. If there are few people in the market area who will buy what you're selling, we say the market is weak.

## POTENTIAL DEMAND

If your business is going to be successful, there must be a market for your product or service and this market must be large enough to support you. If your business is going to be the first of its kind in the market area, this may be hard to judge. For example, you may not believe it, but when we were in High School there was not one pizzeria in our home town. The first pizzeria opened while we were in college. That pizzeria failed. It went out of business because it was not successful in establishing a demand for pizza. A few years ago, we worked with a young couple who wanted to start a new business, but they did not know what kind of business they wanted. The only thing they were sure of, was that they wanted to deal with the students at the local University. They looked around, talked to some students, and discovered that there were 18 pizzerias in town, and, all of them were doing well. To make a long story, short, they started another pizzeria and were an instant success.

Do you see the difference in the situations? The first pizzeria had to create a demand for its product. Very few people in the community knew what pizza was. That meant that in order to be successful, the business had to teach people about its product, then it had to make them believe that they wanted to buy it. In the second case, almost everyone in the market knew about pizza and liked it. That meant that to be successful the business just had to do a better job than its competitors were doing. It did not have to create a demand or educate the market.

This is a very important point to keep in mind when deciding what you're going to sell. If your product or service is new to the people you will be selling it to, you must plan how you intend to teach them about it and how you are going to make them want to buy it. If, on the other hand, the product or service is well known in the market area, then your task is quite different. Instead of having to educate people and create a demand, all you have to do is tap the demand which already exists. To do that, you must learn how your competitors operate and then plan to make your business distinct in some way so that people will prefer to buy from you rather than your competitors. In other words, you just have to do a better job than your competitors are doing.

Creating a market may be possible if there is a demand in the market area which is not being met well. For example, if you lived in a small community which had no movie theater, you might very well be successful in starting a theater. There might be a great many people who are driving to the city to go to the movies. Or, there might be lots of people who would go to the movies if there were a theater in town. You could tap into both groups of people.

On the other hand, if you wanted to start the first store selling audio and sound equipment in that same small community, you might not be successful. Can you see the difference? In any area the proportion of people who go to the movies tends to be greater than the proportion of people who buy audio equipment. If that holds true in your community, then there is likely to be a larger market for movies than for audio equipment.

This is an important point. A few years ago, a man came to see us and wanted help in starting a new business. He had found a vacant lot on the edge of town which was available at a good price and which had good highway access. He wanted to buy that lot and build a roller skating rink. Now, you must realize that this fellow was from an extremely small town in rural Mississippi. The town had a population of about 5,000 people and was located some 60 miles from a city of 75,000. In the nearby city, there were two roller skating rinks and both seemed to be surviving.

Our client was convinced that a skating rink would be successful in his home town because so many of the local high school kids drove to the city on weekends to skate. Not only would he be closer, he could considerably undercut the prices charged in the city as well.

He had done some research and knew what it would cost to build a rink the size he desired as well as to pave the parking lot, to put up a sign and other costs. Together with the cost of the land, he needed $250,000. He wanted us to help him put together an SBA loan package to get the money because his local bank had said no to the loan. The U.S. Small Business Administration has a program which can help small businesses in borrowing money. The important point now is the problem with the market for this business venture.

We didn't like the idea at all. In the first place, we just could not believe that the folks in that small town wanted a skating rink. There was one big plant in town which employed most of them and the local economy was not strong. In the second place, the client had no conception of break even. He was sure that he would have no problems because his wife and children were going to work in the rink, and he would run it on weekends when he was off work from the plant which meant that it wouldn't cost much to operate the rink. Plus, he would be able to keep his job until the place was established. We forced him to do some cost estimation for operating the rink and to forecast his own salary and then we prepared a break even analysis.

Break even analysis is a very important concept. It is important to know that the analysis can give you an estimate of how many customers you will need in order for the business to survive. In this case, the analysis told us that our client would need 250 skaters each week in order to survive. We just didn't think that was feasible in his town. He wouldn't believe us. He got someone else to help him and he actually got a loan and he built the skating rink. The sad part of the story is that now there is a nice new building with hardwood floors for sale in his town. You see, the business failed.

Can you see the problem? Our client knew that a good number of the high school kids drove to the city on weekends to skate. He was convinced that he could attract them to his rink. He did, but there just weren't enough of them, skating frequently enough, to make the business a success. Sadly, he was a perfect example of why your own opinion about the marketability of a business venture can be the wrong opinion. In other words, when you start a business venture, it really does not matter what you want or like or prefer; it matters what a significant number of people in your market area want or like or prefer.

Let's talk about that pizzeria that we mentioned in the last chapter. The pizzeria is an example of exactly the right way to choose a product and start a business. What happened was that a young couple just out of college called us up and asked for help in starting a restaurant. They said that they had selected our town because it had a large university which was growing and would provide a steady source of new patrons. We talked about what kind of restaurant they wanted and they said they hadn't decided yet. They wanted to look at the local competition and locations which might be available.

We found several good places located close to the university, several within walking distance of some of the larger dorms. We also found that there were 18 pizzerias in town, that being the single most frequently encountered type of restaurant. Our clients checked out every one of those, and all of them seemed to be doing fine. Our clients decided to go with pizza. They settled on a place, leased it, and put $20,000 into leasehold improvements. The place was built for students. They had three different rooms set up, each with a juke box and lined with booths. The only tables were long, common tables, laid out down the center of two of the rooms. The third room had arcade games between the booths.

Inside three months, they had surpassed their sales forecast for the entire first year. The place was a resounding success. Now they have three restaurants and two arcades scattered about the edges of the campus. For two kids in their twenties, they are an impressive pair.

Do you see the difference in their approach? The people in this last example went about everything the right way. They chose a location carefully. They studied the market and the competition and they made a careful plan. They were able to be successful because they understood the people they were trying to attract and knew what they had to do. They also made sure there were enough people in the market area to make their business successful.

## THE UNDERLYING SATISFACTION

In reality, what people are really buying may not be obvious. You might think that the young couple in the last example sell pizza and sandwiches. That's what they make their money on, but that's not what they're really selling. When students come in to the restaurant, they usually join a group of people who are already there. Can you guess what they are really selling? It's entertainment. The students see the restaurant as a gathering place for their friends. They can listen to music, play arcade games, and, incidently, they can eat.

This is one of the reasons why it is important for you to know so much about your product or service, your customers, and the market area. That knowledge makes it easier for you to understand what will be successful and how you have to go about setting up your business.

Let's say that you wanted to start a martial arts school. Perhaps you know karate and would like to start a business because you love it so much. We know two different people who started martial arts schools. One was successful and the other was not. The difference was that one knew what he was selling. He understood the market well and he designed his school carefully to match what the market wanted. You see, what he was really selling was not martial arts training. It was self confidence. He built his program around that idea. Students spent time in meditation, learned to be extremely polite to each other and to everyone else they met. They read and studied about martial arts, and concentrated on learning how to control their bodies. Most of his students were young: 10 to 15 years old. The business was successful because there were a large number of people in the market area, in that age bracket, who really wanted to gain self confidence.

The other fellow thought he was teaching people how to fight. He built his program around fighting competitions and concentrated on teaching people to be more successful in the fighting matches and tournaments. He attracted a goodly number of students in the beginning. Most of them were a little older: 18 to 25. But, there just weren't enough people in his market area, in that age bracket, who truly wanted to master fighting techniques, and his business failed. However, please note that his failure did NOT mean that his concept would not work. It just would not work in the market area in which he established the business. If he had started his business in some other area, he might have been successful.

## THE ROLE OF KNOWLEDGE

Choosing a product or service requires you to have knowledge about that product or service, about the market area, and about the people who will be buying from you. It's all tied together. We're going to talk more about the market area in the next chapter. We will also have more to say about the people. Right now, we want you to concentrate on the product or service. How do you learn about it? How do you gain the knowledge that you will need?

The best approach is to have experience with the product or service you intend to sell. If you have worked in a business which sold the same or similar things, then you will know much more about them than if you don't have such experience. That means that a good way to prepare for starting your own business is to work for someone else in a business similar to the one you want to start. It's almost like an apprenticeship. It's a great way to learn, especially if you know that you will start a business yourself someday. Your plan will make you watch closely to learn all you can about every aspect of the business. It's also a good way to get the money you're going to need. You can save it while you're learning.

You've probably heard stories about fortunes made by people who invented something entirely new. The truth is that many inventors are not successful. We just don't hear about the failures very often. There are exceptions, of course, but most of the real success stories are about people who had a great deal of knowledge and used that knowledge to figure out a new way of doing things. They usually have a good plan for how they are going to build their businesses and they work hard. One of the most famous success stories is about Stephen Jobs and Steve Wozniak who started the Apple Computer Company. The story goes that they sold an old Volkswagen for $2,000 and used that money to start the first business making personal computers. The company became the fastest growing business in history. Today, of course, the company is huge and both Steves became extremely wealthy. The real story is that the two young men worked for computer companies, Hewlett Packard and Atari, and learned a great deal about the insides of computers. They had an idea to use that knowledge to build a very small, inexpensive machine. It was a great idea, but it was based on the knowledge they had gained about how computers worked. They used their money to build a prototype, a computer like the one they wanted to manufacture, then they took that idea to several wealthy people and tried to get them to invest. To make a long story short, they got some help and sold a man with a long history of experience in the computer business on the idea of joining them. Mark Markkula joined them and was able to raise $1 million dollars to get the business started. Markkula became the President of the company and ran it while the two Steves gained more knowledge and experience by working with him. That may not sound as romantic as the popular version of the story, but it is more real. Don't forget that if the two Steves hadn't had the original idea, nothing would have happened. The idea just needed a good plan and some hard work to make it pay off. Most ideas are like that.

So, if you want to have a successful business some day, watch, study and learn. We're going to help you with that last part. While we do, keep thinking about products or services. Think about things you find interesting, things you know something about, things you think might sell. Try out those ideas to see if they are marketable as you learn more about the process of starting and managing a business. Marketable simply means salable. Can you sell it to people? Can you build a business around the idea? Will you have to educate people about the idea? Can you make a business that will be distinctive to sell it? How can you market it?

## HIGH TECH VENTURES

Many people have the idea that the only businesses which can be successful are high tech businesses, so you have to be a technology guru in order to start a venture. Nothing could be farther from the truth. The most successful entrepreneur is history is actually one of the less well know figures. His name is Wayne Huizenga, and he is the only person in history to build three Fortune

1000 companies. His story is really typical of a really successful entrepreneur. After a tour of duty in the U.S. Army, he dropped out of college to go to work for a friend who owned a garbage collection company. Two years later, he bought his own truck and launched his own garbage collection business. Huizenga was legendary for his hard work. When first starting out, he would drive the truck from 2:30 AM until noon, then spend the rest of the day knocking on doors and introducing himself to drum up new business. He grew the company to 40 trucks, then he merged with another garbage collection business, and formed Waste Management, Inc. He took that firm public and used equity capital from the stock market to buy 150 other local and regional garbage services, making WMI the largest waste disposal company in the U.S. It soon grew to become one of the 1,000 largest companies in the world.

Great entrepreneurs don't just start businesses, they see potential that others do not see. In 1987, Huizenga and two partners bought a video rental business called Blockbuster. Following the same model as the WMI success, he took Blockbuster public in 1989. He grew the company from $7 million in sales and 19 stores in 1989, to $4 billion in sales with 3,700 stores in 11 countries in 1994, making it one of the 1,000 largest businesses in the world. Incidentally, he sold the business for $8.4 billion in 1994.

Huizenga was far from finished. He created AutoNation, the first U.S. wide auto dealer, and the first to ever go public. He grew it wo 370 dealerships, and it, too, became one of the 1,000 largest businesses in the word. Huizenga went on to establish Extended Stay America, Republic Services and more. He is the only person ever to develop six New York Stock Exchange listed companies. He bought the Miami Dolphins football team, and the Florida Marlins baseball team, and the Panthers hockey team, and became the only person to ever own three pro teams in a single market. Incidentally, two of his teams won national championships.

If you pay attention to the story, you will note that Huizenga never started a single high tech company. He dropped out of college and he knew very little about technology. However, he knew people, and he understood hard work and dedication. A great anecdote about Huizenga has him allegedly giving this piece of advice: "The thing about trash pickup is that when times get tough, you still want me to come to your house and pick up your garbage!"

## THE ROLE OF MARKETING

Whether you are educating people or making your business distinctive, the tool you must use is marketing. Marketing includes advertising, but it is much more than that. Marketing refers to the whole approach which a company can use to sell its products or services.

Harley Procter was a salesman for the family candle, lard and soap company in 1878. The company was called Procter and Gamble. Harley got the job of selling a new, hard, white soap, which the company had developed. Harley called it ivory soap and he decided to advertise the product. He was so successful that he soon caught the attention of the entire business world.

Harley's early efforts laid the groundwork for much of the consumer advertising and marketing techniques which we use today. Procter and Gamble remains one of the largest advertisers in the world. In fact, they do so much advertising in day time television that many of those programs are called soap operas. Harley learned a great deal about why people buy things and he used that knowledge to plan his marketing efforts. That's still the secret to an effective marketing effort. In a later chapter, we will be talking about why people buy things. Understanding something about people is the first step in building a marketing plan.

**REVIEW**

Remember that time and distance are important considerations today so that having a better product or service than our competitors does not mean that the world will seek us out. So what do we do?

We plan carefully. We choose a product or service with which we are familiar, which is appropriate to the market in which we are interested, or we choose another, more appropriate location. Home towns may not be large enough to support our selection of product or service.

Familiarity or experience helps in the choice, but common sense is also an important factor in deciding what to sell as well as where to sell it. Remember the distinction between creating or tapping an existing demand. The former may be much more difficult for a new business, but more rewarding in the long term. Can you wait for success?

Know what you are really selling and plan to learn all you can about your product or service. Watch, study and learn, are the key aspects of success; then, plan.

Remember that the most successful businesses and the most successful entrepreneurs in history have not been high tech firms. You have to know your market and you have to know what you are selling, but you don't need to be an inventor to be successful.

## QUESTIONS, EXERCISES AND CASES

### Questions

1. There is a quote from a well-known individual. Comment upon it and indicate why it is applicable for entrepreneurs. Can you give an example which might support the quotation?

   *If a man can write a better book, preach a better sermon, or make a better mouse trap than his neighbor, though he builds his house in the woods, the world will make a beaten path to his door. (Emerson)*

2. Why is your own personal judgement about the marketability of an item invalid?

3. Define the following terms:

   a. Product
   b. Service
   c. Product mix
   d. Demand
   e. Market
   f. Marketing

### Exercises

1. Notice several products and/or services in your neighborhood and see if you can ascertain why people buy that particular product or service. Are they using the best approach? Would you do something differently? If it were your business, what would you do?

2. Create an initial strategy for your product or service. Indicate what it is and how you plan to market it. Present your idea to others and see what they think. Remember we usually think that our friends see things the same as we (that's why we are friends), but do we have enough to make our idea successful?

**Case**

We were called in as consultants by the owner of a small lounge in coastal Alabama. The owner, who was operating the lounge as a proprietorship, had been open for 6 months and had been losing money steadily during that time. The lounge was located in a small town which was 50 miles from the nearest city and which was dominated by the shrimp fishing industry. We went to see the owner at the lounge on a Friday night. It was located on the main drag, 3 or 4 miles from the center of the little town. We passed by another lounge on the way out which had a parking lot filled with cars.

When we got there we were really impressed with the place. It was beautiful! The owner said he had invested $20,000 in leasehold improvements in the place and I don't doubt it. The building was well done, both inside and outside. It had a long padded bar, a carpeted floor space with circular tables and padded chairs, a hardwood dance floor and a raised stage for musicians. Live music was featured on Friday and Saturday nights. No big names, but good players who featured contemporary 'pop' music. The bar served several kinds of beer on tap, wine, mixed drinks and snacks. No food was served except for a weekly oyster bash on Tuesday nights featuring fresh oysters and shrimp. Prices seemed to us to be reasonable. Not cheap, but not too expensive either. He had a bartender and two waitresses who were clean, well dressed and polite. They were all young. The bartender was wearing a tie.

There were a few customers in the lounge and they all seemed to be enjoying themselves. They were young, couples mostly, and were all dressed nicely.

The owner said that this lounge had been a dream of his for years. He had always wanted to own a really nice place, not what he called a *honky tonk*. He had finally saved enough money to make the venture, but he was not a wealthy man and he could not continue to put money into the business. He had tried all kinds of specials and all kinds of advertising, but he couldn't seem to make a profit. He had talked to customers at great length, but all of them said they loved the place and wouldn't change a thing. That's why he had called us. He was on the verge of losing the place.

We talked to him and the employees, looked at the books, watched the customers for a while and left. We told him we'd get back to him soon. On the way out of town we stopped by that other lounge we had passed to look at his competition. The place was jumping! It had a juke box, blaring so loud you couldn't hear a thing. It was packed with people, most of whom were wearing work clothes. The place wasn't nearly as nice as our client's, and honestly wasn't terribly clean. Our client's problem suddenly became crystal clear.

Describe the problem in this case and indicate what you would do?

# CHAPTER FOUR

## CHOOSING A LOCATION

### INTRODUCTION

The *market area* is that geographic territory from which you can expect sales to come. That's usually the community, town, city or county where you locate your business. Most people starting a new venture do not pay enough attention to the issue of area selection. All too often they simply start a business in their home towns. That may not be a good idea. There has to be a market for your product or service in the market area. There have to be people who will want to buy, and who are able to buy, what you're selling; and there have to be enough of those people to make your business successful. Both the willing and able parts are important.

### THE DANGERS OF A HOMETOWN LOCATION

We knew a lady who was well known in a small town as an excellent chef. She had long wanted to start her own restaurant. She finally got the chance when a restaurant in a city 30 miles away went up for sale. She bought the restaurant and started to work. She specialized in gourmet dishes and the business was a success. She even had many friends from the local area drive over to her restaurant from time to time. Everyone agreed that the place was wonderful and that she was doing a fantastic job.

There was one problem. The long drive to and from work was a problem for her. The restaurant was only open for dinner but cleaning after closing and getting ready to open again meant that she had to leave to go to work at 2:00 in the afternoon and didn't get home until 1:00 in the morning. To make matters worse, her husband worked in construction and had to get up early each morning to go to work. This went on for a year. It didn't make for a happy home life and her husband was really upset about it. So, she decided to move the restaurant.

She found a location back home in the small community where she lived and moved her restaurant there. The first week all of her friends came to the restaurant. Everyone was happy she was back and the food was wonderful. In six months, she was out of business.

Everyone agreed that the place was great and the food wonderful, but they all went to eat there only about once a month. Being gourmet, the restaurant was expensive and so it was a place to go on special occasions or for a special treat. That kind of operation needs a large population base to support it. There just weren't enough people in the small community to support a gourmet restaurant.

There can be other problems with your hometown, even if there is a market which can support your business. The local economy might be a problem. We are familiar with a business which failed in its first year of operation because the owner didn't think about the local economy. The business was located in a rural county in North Carolina which had one major employer. That employer was a paper mill which had been in business for more than 40 years and had more than 5,000 employees. Over the last 10 years, the paper mill had been coming under attack because of water pollution claims. In fact, the Environmental Protection Agency (the EPA) had threatened to close the plant if it did not reduce the level of its discharges into the local river. Political pressure was brought to bear, the plant spent considerable dollars in pollution control, and the EPA was satisfied for the time being.

Like most people, our client had decided to go into business in his hometown. It never occurred to him to wonder what would happen if the paper mill got into trouble. He had been in business less than six months when the EPA hammer fell. Pressure from environmental groups had been building and the EPA decided to require that the mill update its pollution controls further. The management of the mill declared that it was not economically feasible to upgrade such an old facility; so, they cut back on the plant operations and reduced pollution in that way. The result of this cut back was a lay off of more than 3,000 workers. In a county with a population of 30,000 people and virtually no other industry which could absorb this layoff, the effects were devastating. Our client was only one of many firms to fail in the ripple effects.

Obviously, a prospective business owner would think twice about starting a business in an area that was having trouble. Our client just didn't think about it because there were no problems at the time he got ready to open his business. All the signs were there. He should have thought about it. It was clear that problems with the EPA were highly possible. It simply never occurred to him. Like many people planning to start a business, he never considered starting it anywhere but in his home town. He didn't think there was any decision to be made. Well, there **is** a decision to make, and it's an important one; perhaps, critical.

## AREA PREREQUISITES

The kind of business you intend to start will determine the kind of area you want. There are three important factors. First, the area must have a large enough number of people who will be your customers to support your business which means that you need to know who the customers for your business are going to be. Second, those people must be able to buy what you're selling which means that they must have the income level to afford to buy. Finally, the outlook for the future needs to be good. That is, you want both the number of people and their ability to buy to stay where you need it.

Beyond the general needs, a particular kind of business might have special needs. For a manufacturing business, you might need a supply of trained workers and good transportation systems. For a construction company, you might want good population growth which will mean lots of new home building. For other firms, the legal environment could be a key. One client of ours selected the Atlanta, Georgia area to start a local delivery trucking company. He found out that the city required trucks delivering within the city limits to have a special permit, and the city wouldn't issue new permits because there were too many trucks driving around town. Our client located a trucking company whose owner wanted to retire. He bought that company just so he could get the delivery permit. Finally, he was in business.

In another case, we saw a business owner start a grocery store. He bought land and began to construct the building. Then, he learned that the city limits were about 1,000 feet short of his location. The county prohibited the sale of beer and wine. This was a major setback because the other grocery stores in town could sell beer and wine, giving them a competitive edge.

## SOURCES OF INFORMATION

There are many publications available which can give you information about an area and help you in selecting an area for your business. Most of this information is available free or at a small charge. In the U.S., the Census Bureau publishes manuals which have basic demographic data about every area in the country. Demographic data means the number of people living in each area. This information is broken down by age, race, sex, family size, and family income. The Bureau also includes a great deal of information about the number and kinds of businesses in an area as well as things like unemployment rates and other things which could be important. All of this information is available in most libraries. The governments of most nations also tabulate demographic information about their populations, and make it available.

The American Small Business Administration also produces publications designed to help find an area. One of the publications available from the SBA is a report which shows the number of people who are needed in an area to support a particular kind of business. Combine that information with a population count from the Census Bureau and you will have a much better idea of whether a particular area will support your business. You can call the SBA office in Washington, D.C. to find out how to get this information. International counterparts of the U.S. SBA exist in many nations. You just have to take the time to look for information. The internet has become a tremendous resource for such information.

SBDCs (Small Business Development Centers) are located at many universities around the United States and Small Business Centers (SBCs) are located in many American Community Colleges. They can be of tremendous help in start-up planning for your business. Their help is generally free. You can find the location of the nearest SBDC from the SBA office in Washington or ask at your local community college for an SBC. Colleges and schools around the world share the U.S. model of projecting a community development and assistance mission, and can be great sources of information and support, regardless of where you are located.

There is help available in the U.S. at the state level. In fact, all of the states have a business development office. The purpose of these offices is to provide information to people who are thinking about starting a business in the state. These offices collect business and demographic data which can help in choosing a state and in choosing a region in that state for your business. To get this information, you can contact the office of business development in the state capital.

Finally, information is available in most towns and cities in American and throughout the world through local sources. Chambers of Commerce collect data of interest to businesses and are always happy to help someone who is thinking about starting a new business. The local employment security commission can help you find prospective employees and can give you information about unemployment levels, skill levels of the work force, nature and number of employers in the area, and a host of other factors. The local zoning board can also be a gold mine of information. Not only will it be able to show you where various types of industry can be located, it can show you where your competitors will be. The zoning board can also give you ideas about locations which might be good for your business. Finding local information can be challenging, but you will find that local bankers are good sources, especially loan officers specializing in commercial loans.

Don't overlook personal research. In the pizza example, the owners conducted a survey of the competition by personally visiting every pizza restaurant in town. They looked the place over, bought dinner, watched the customers, evaluated the service, hours, location and menu of every competitor. As a matter of fact, they continue to do this on a regular basis today. There is no substitute for personal investigation.

## PSYCHOGRAPHIC DATA

As we have discussed, psychographics are characteristics of your target market which are based on the desires, interests and preferences of a subset of a demographic sector. We talked about fans of particular types of music, and people interested in supporting the "green" movement. There are no real sources of data to help you identify the numbers of people in a given market area who embody a particular set of psychographics, however, such information could be crucial. You must garner information yourself through your personal research.

Let's say that you are interested in creating a business to cater to collectors of antique weapons and firearms. We know of a very successful venture which does exactly that. Our first impression is that such collectors are rare because this is an expensive hobby, and one which does not have broad appeal in most market areas. Our second impression is that obtaining inventory for such a venture would be quite challenging. First, it would be expensive, and secondly, it would be hard to find, as most of the pieces we might want to see would already be housed in a museum or in a private collection. How could we handle these challenges? The company we are describing decided to concentrate on making a market for sellers and buyers, rather than acquiring inventory itself, and it decided to pursue a national market base. It established an auction business. It took several years, and early years involved heavy advertising in selected magazines and journals, but the venture was able to establish itself as one of the premier auction sites for vintage weapons in the United States, and collectors come from around the world to participate in its auctions, just as other collectors, or the estates of collectors, choose the company to liquidate their holdings.

The moral of this story is that from a psychographic perspective, you can choose the target market you want to attract, but you might have to be creative to establish a venture which can have access to sufficient numbers of your target to be viable. Sometimes, it takes a leap of faith. There is a locally owned grocery store in our area that sells only natural foods. It does not stock anything that has artificial ingredients or which was raised or produced with the use of hormones, drugs, or other such aids. It was the first store of its kind in the area, but it caught on, and now has a huge following. People drive for 30 miles, past many traditional grocery stores to shop there. The owner once told us that he just "knew" it would be a success. That is intuition! You just need to understand that intuition needs knowledge to work. Researching your market, your area, your processes and prospects will feed that intuition, and you may come to use it to make your final decisions about a great many things.

## FACTORS IN THE SELECTION

Once you have settled on an area, you have to find an actual location for your business. You will have to know something about what you need. This includes the physical size of the building and any special needs inside the building like kitchen equipment or display counters. You can't simply go to real estate agents and find a place to rent which you think you can afford. This is absolutely the wrong way to go about finding a location. The first question which any real estate agent will ask is "How large a place do you need?" Until you can answer that basic question, there is no need to begin looking.

The first thing you have to do is decide how important the location of the business is going to be. For example, if you plan to open a fudge shop, you will probably want to locate where there will be a lot of people passing by your shop. The location of your business will be a critical factor in whether it will be successful. It may be that the best place for you will be in a shopping mall. The location could be so important that you will want to find a place and gear everything else to its size. You can't sell fishing worms and live bait in the middle of the city. You can sell them quite well beside the lake. In other words, location can be everything. You will want to find a place first. After that, the number of people you will employ, the amount of inventory you can carry, the number and size of display cases, everything, has to be planned to fit into the available space which you have found.

On the other hand, it might be that the location is not very important at all. For example, if you plan to start a construction company and you never expect people to actually come to your office, where you locate will not be important. In this case, you will want to decide how much space you need to store your tools, equipment, building materials, supplies, and so forth. Then, you will look for the cheapest place that has what you need.

It could be that drive by traffic is what is important. If you plan to open a dry cleaners, you will probably want to have a location which has a lot of drive by traffic so that you will be located conveniently for as many people as possible.

Even if you won't need access to a lot of foot traffic or drive by traffic, the location could be very important. For example, if you plan to start a law practice, the location of your office will have a major impact on your image; what people think about your business. A location in a nice office building, in a nice section of town will send a clear message to your clients. The same thing is true of a location in an old house in a run-down neighborhood which has been converted to an office. Unfortunately, the message you are sending in this case is quite different.

You have to decide just how important the location is going to be. If the location is going to be the primary method which you are going to use to attract customers, it will be crucial. If the location is only part of the approach you are going to use to attract customers, it is important but not crucial. If your customers will never see your location, then it is unimportant. For a crucial location, you will want to choose the place first, then build everything else around that. In other situations, you will want to decide how big a place you require and any other special needs you may have.

## DETERMINING SPACE REQUIREMENTS

If you are going to start a retail store, a store which will sell directly to people who come in, the size of the store you will need is determined by how much inventory you will carry. Inventory means the products you will be displaying in your store. You've probably been in stores when you felt crowded because there was too much inventory in too small a space. That's a problem. The reverse situation is a problem, too. If there's not enough inventory to look good in the store, it may look empty to customers and they could leave without looking around or buying anything. So, you will want to study how much space inventory takes up and how much of it you will need.

Let's say you want to open a store selling sporting goods. Go look at all the sporting goods stores you can find. What do they carry and how much space does it take up? Pay attention to how the inventory is displayed. Do they use racks set in rows out in the floor? Do they keep some things in glass display cases? How big are the racks and cases? Now think about what you want to sell. How many baseball bats will you have on hand? They come in a large variety of styles, lengths and weights. Do you need one of every type? How important will baseball bats be to your store? Will you be making more money on football equipment or will baseball equipment be the primary thing you expect to sell? Can you just stock a few bats and order anything else a customer wants? How will you display those bats and how much space will they take up? You have to follow this process with everything you intend to sell.

As you work your way through the inventory, you will begin to get a picture of what your store should look like. Make a floor plan. Lay out the store on paper. Draw it to scale and fill in areas with display racks and cases. Draw in the racks and cases to scale. Put in a cash register and think about how people will move around through the store. Leave room for walkways and think about how people will come in and out of your store. Move things around to see if you like that layout better.

Look at that layout again. Do you have room to grow? What if you need to add more inventory items as time goes by? What if the store grows? You will want to leave enough room to handle growth, at least for a while. You will probably have to sign a lease. That's an agreement to rent the space for a specified period of time at a particular rent amount. Leases are often for five years. This can mean that you won't be able to move your business for the term of the lease. That's why you need to think about room for more inventory or for growth.

This part of the planning for a new business can be a lot of fun. Let's say you want to open a restaurant. You will want to look at as many restaurants as you can. Then, you will begin laying out your tables and the kitchen on paper and visualizing what it will look like. Think about decorations you might use. Where will they go? This is the general process you will follow for any business you start.

The layout of the business well help you determine how much space you need. Then, when you actually find a location, you can go back to your layout and make changes to fit the space at which you are looking. It can help you decide whether this location will work for you. Once you have decided on a place, you can finalize the layout and this will help you to determine the kinds of furniture and fixtures you will need. Fixtures are the counters, display racks and display cases and things like that. The layout will also help you to see the equipment you will want, like stoves and ovens, or other things you will need to set up the business.

In addition to considering the layout of the business, before signing a lease, it would be wise to consider the geographic area in which you are locating. Short term leases will be more expensive than long term leases; however, long term leases can be costly in other ways. For instance, a ten year lease might be attractive from a financial perspective, but if the demographics of the area in which you have located change dramatically in that ten year period, then you could find yourself in a declining neighborhood which might well be inconsistent with your image. Geographic areas change as well as people. Think about the trend away from downtown areas to malls. That change killed many businesses and changes such as that continue to occur. Strip shopping centers may be influenced by the businesses which locate in or near them and you may or may not have any control over who locates there.

## THE ROLE OF COST

There is generally a trade off between cost and location. The better a location is, the more it will cost to rent it. A place with more foot traffic passing by will cost more to rent than a place with less foot traffic. That means that malls generally cost more than shopping centers which cost more than shops on the street downtown. Shops in malls and shopping centers are rented by the square foot of floor space and the cost per foot is higher in some parts of the mall than in other parts. This is a result of the variation in foot traffic around the mall. In fact, malls often charge a flat amount per square foot plus a percentage of your sales on top of that.

When we leave malls and shopping centers, rent costs tend to vary according to the traffic flows from people driving by. Locations on major roads generally cost more than locations on side roads. The principle is the same as for foot traffic. More potential customers passing by means more rent.

So you see, a cheaper location is not necessarily better. As we discussed in the previous section, the decision is based on how important the location is to your business. If location will be a key factor in your success, you might very well be better off paying more for your location because the more expensive places will give you access to more potential customers.

## SPECIAL NEEDS

Many businesses have special needs that the location must satisfy. A trucking company may need to locate near major highways or interstates. If you are going to sell satellite receiver antennae, you will need a sky line which will allow you to draw in the right satellite signals. If you are going to open a gas station and restaurant appealing to truckers, you will need wide enough roads and parking lots for tractor-trailer rigs to be able to get in and out of your place. Some kinds of manufacturing companies need large quantities of water. Other businesses might need access to an airport, a train station, or to public transportation.

Special needs also include zoning permits. In most cities and larger communities, the land has been divided into zones. Each zone can only have certain types of businesses. For example, if you wanted to open a mobile home park, you might find that lots of areas were closed to you by the zoning regulations. The same thing could happen if you wanted to open a garage to repair cars. In fact, zoning regulations can affect almost any kind of business you can imagine. You can find out about zoning regulations from the local city or county zoning board or planning commission.

Determining the special needs of a business may be as simple as exercising your common sense. If you want to build vacation homes to sell, you can't put them next to a busy airport. If you're going to open a kennel and board dogs, you can't open your business in the middle of a housing development.

## LOCATING IN THE HOME

A lot of people think about locating at home, at least for a while, until the business gets up and going. If customers aren't going to be coming to your place, this might be a good idea. It could be inexpensive, quick and easy. Obviously, you can't stay at home if the location is going to be important to the success of your business.

You will need to make sure that there are no zoning regulations which prevent you from starting the business at home. Many cities will not allow businesses to be run in a neighborhood. If you are going to have customers coming to your house, you need to make sure they will feel comfortable and not be ill at ease because they are in your home.

Professionals such as accountants may well become home-based businesses, because much of the work is done on a computer and without the necessity of the client's presence for long periods of time. However, retail outlets should be discouraged. At a recent lecture, a lady approached us about her business. She sold expensive, pageant gowns for very young girls who entered beauty contests. She said that everyone loved her products, but her business was not doing very well. When we learned that she was selling the dresses out of her home, we asked where in the home the business was located and whether the customers called for appointments. She told us that she had a sign on the door that said, "Come on in." All you had to do was walk down the hall of her home to a back bedroom where all of her inventory was displayed. We suggested that many people would be concerned about just walking into someone's home unannounced and traveling through thc house to find the desired inventory. We felt that if she really wanted to be successful, she should move out of her home or, refusing that on the basis of expense, that she convert the garage to the retail area, as have many rural beauty salons.

While home-based businesses are not out of the question, you need to consider the comfort of your customers. For professionals, meeting customers at appointed times might well be acceptable. Yet having constant flows of customers into one's home might be uncomfortable for the customer as well as the family. Think of your market and your image, then decide if locating in your home is advisable.

## MAKING THE FINAL CHOICE

First, choose an area. Think about places you would like to live and investigate whether they can support your business. When you have chosen an area, look for where the competition is located. Sometimes it is good to be located close to competitors so that you can piggyback off the traffic which they draw. That's why fast food restaurants tend to locate near each other and it is the basic reason that shopping centers and malls developed. Think about the size place you need and make a list of alternative sites. Get out and look at all of them. What are the good points and the bad points about each location? Consider as many alternatives as you can before making a final selection. The site you finally select is going to be with you for a while. Make sure it's the right one for your business.

Find out about leases available and lease terms. Think about the effect of each alternative location on the image you want the business to have in the minds of its customers. The site which you finally select is a major part of that image. If you are opening a professional services business, then a prestigious office address may be important to support the right image. If you are opening a discount retail business, an address in a shopping mall could be a disadvantage because it carries with it the image of expensive stores.

Be sure to allow for change or growth in your business in the site selection as well. Try to visualize what the business will be like in a year or two if it is successful. We worked with one store selling drinks and snacks. The owner chose a fine location in a shopping center, and signed a five year lease. The store was located in the middle of the strip of shops. That meant that the store could not have drive-up service. The business grew and within about two years, customers began to want drive-up service. That meant that the business had to relocate. The landlord would not let our client out of the lease without paying a substantial penalty for canceling the lease early. That penalty could have been avoided, because at the time of the original lease, a corner location was available in that same shopping center. Our client chose not to take the corner store because it had a higher rental than the interior store location. Our client had tried to save a few dollars and ended up spending much more.

## REVIEW

The market area, site and physical location of a business is important to the success of that business. Many potential business owners tend to look close to home and feel that what they prefer is marketable to others.

Population density, repeat business, the local economy and environmental regulations are often overlooked as factors which could influence the success or failure of a business. In addition, you need to know the number of people, their ability to buy and future prospects before determining the market area.

An important consideration in determining the location for the business is the necessity for special requirements such as permits, space or transportation. Changing demographics are a consideration as well.

There are many sources of information about any given market area and most are readily available at local libraries or Chamber of Commerce offices. Other good sources for demographic data are the Census Bureau, the Small Business Administration, the Small Business Development Center at a University, a Small Business Center at the Community College, or their international counterparts. A more exciting source of data is personal observation and research. Only this later research tool can help you determine the viability of a psychographic market segment.

After determining how important the location of the business is, then physical size and needs such as special equipment and displays must be determined. Inventory considerations must be explored as part of the size and display needs.

Cost considerations as well as foot traffic and drive by traffic are important parts of the location decision. Since special requirements such as permits and zoning regulations play a role in the choice of a location, these influence the viability of locating your business in your home.

Remember, first choose an area, examine the competition, consider the space requirements, and look at alternative sites. Consider available leases, the potential for growth and the image you want your business to have. Don't forget that the image of the business is a reflection on you and your ability to plan well. Be as careful in determining the market area as you are in choosing your product or service.

## QUESTIONS, EXERCISES AND CASES

### Questions

1. Why is your own personal judgement about the marketability of an item invalid?

2. What aspects must be considered in home-based businesses? Home town businesses?

3. What is market area and why is its selection important?

4. Why is your choice of products/services and market area iterative?

5. What are some of the considerations in determining site selection for your business?

6. What are factors which are often overlooked in making location decisions and how does that impact the success or failure of a business

7. Define the following terms:

   a. market area
   b. demographics
   c. inventory
   d. lease
   e. image

8. Why are size of location as well as cost so important to location determination? Give an example of both good and bad choices from your own observation.

### Exercises

1. Decide upon a product or service for your type of business. Then graph a layout to give you a better feel for your location needs. Be sure in include any interior or exterior views.

2. Look at the businesses in the area which you feel are appropriate for your business or just examine the area and see whether you feel that those businesses made the right location choices.

## Case

The Ultimate opened its doors early last year. It was the ultimate college hangout: *the* place for good food, fun, friends, and variety. It had a menu of pizza, subs, steaks, lasagna, spaghetti, chili and hamburgers. The owner was young, local, knew everyone, and he was in heaven about his venture.

Opening week had its share of problems. Everyone wanted burgers when Todd expected the Italian cuisine to be the best seller based on his prior experience with a local competitor. He had to suggest alternatives. The help was slow, because they weren't trained, and frustrated diners with class schedules to keep had to bolt their food when it came.

The decor was romantic with red and white checkered table cloths for the booths and low lighting. Actually, there was a problem with the lighting. It was either off or on. On was very bright and off was dark. Todd wanted a romantic atmosphere for dates and dinners, so he placed filters in the light panels allowing only a very small amount of light to come through. Some of the customers were heard to remark to the waitresses that the food was very good but they wished that they could have seen it. Ordering from the menu was an adventure. Customers were seen striking matches to read. When several of the older customers asked Todd about candles, he claimed that they were too expensive and the students would swipe them.

The food was delicious and the prices were reasonable for the quantity served. The portions were large but many a diner was surprised by the low bill. The variety should please everyone. And there were specials from time to time, usually lasagna or all you can eat spaghetti. But occasionally there was ribeye steak. The only difficulty for the patrons was that they didn't know when the specials were coming. The advertisement was on the chalkboard inside the restaurant.

Newcomers were told of this great place to eat just off campus, but most couldn't find it and ended up at the Pizza Hut a few yards down the road. The Ultimate was parallel to the main drag, but you had to know it was there. It was connected to a service station and was not readily differentiated from the garage. The gas pumps and tow truck parked near by faked out potential customers.

Too soon, the school year was over. Todd was in a quandary as to whether he should close down or stay open. He didn't have the same number of customers but many of the locals were hoping that he would stay open. Professors and students with late classes went there for a while and then discovered that Todd was closing early. There was no knowing the hours. Soon he was closing at lunch and open only from 4 PM to 10 PM. Many of his best customers were no longer coming in. What could he do?

1. What are some of the obvious problems you can deduce from the case?

2. Describe the location. Why would Todd have chosen it? What are potential advantages and disadvantages for such a location?

3. Were there any inconsistencies in image both obviously and reading between the lines?

4. What was Todd's target market and how was he planning to compete?

5. Is this enterprise headed toward success or failure? Why or why not?

# CHAPTER FIVE

## IDENTIFYING COMPETITORS

### INTRODUCTION

If you go into business, you *will* have competitors. These are the other businesses who will be trying to sell to your customers. Competition is very much a part of business life. In fact, we call it competition because it is so much like a game. You and your competitors are trying to win the game. In business, winning means making the sale. In the game, the competitor who does the best job wins the sale. That's why it's so important for you to learn about your competitors. You play best against people you know. If you know their skills, their abilities, their strengths, and their weaknesses, you can play your best against them. It's like that in business. You need to know your competitors, their strengths and their weaknesses in order to play better against them.

### TYPES OF COMPETITORS

There are two basic types of competitors you must face. A *direct competitor* is another business with which you will be competing 'head to head.' That means a business which carries the same basic items or provides the same basic services as you do. If you run a restaurant, all the other restaurants in town will be your direct competitors because your customers can only eat in one restaurant at a time. If they decide to eat in your restaurant tonight, you win because they can't eat in your competitor's restaurant, at least, not tonight.

Not all restaurants are alike. That means that not all direct competitors are alike. It also means that some competitors will be more of a problem for you than others. For example, if you are selling sandwiches and pizza, then who do you think is your *main* competition? Obviously, another pizzeria will be more competition for you than a hamburger restaurant, although the hamburger restaurant is also a competitor, just not one which is as strong.

You also face competition from businesses which do not sell the same kinds of things as you do. These businesses are called *indirect competitors.* They compete for the dollars which your customers can spend. It's a different kind of competition, but just as real. If you run a movie theater, then other theaters will be direct competitors; but, the bowling alley will be a competitor as well. You are both selling entertainment. People only have so much money they can afford to spend on entertainment in any given week. So, if your customer decides to spend his or her entertainment dollars on bowling this week, that means you lose. The customer can't bowl and go to the movies at the same time.

Indirect competition is more of a problem for some kinds of businesses than for others. If you run a convenience store, you face direct competition from other convenience stores and indirect competition from grocery stores and supermarkets. For you, the indirect competition from grocery stores can be *very* serious. If a grocery store has a location that is just as convenient and decides to stay open 24 hours, that store could destroy your business. If you run a movie theater, then the other movie theaters in town are your direct competitors, but every business in town selling entertainment is an indirect competitor. If you see an increase in the number of entertainment businesses, you should begin to worry. They can dilute the market. Just think what will happen if four new miniature golf courses, three new water slides, two new video stores, a new bowling alley, and two new arcades open up in town. There will be so many entertainment businesses available in the market area that they will hurt each other and you. All of the businesses will attract some customers and all of them compete for the same dollars. That means that your customer draw will shrink and it may drop off so much that it damages your ability to survive.

For other businesses, indirect competition is less of a problem. For some businesses, it is practically nonexistent. If you run a ladies' dress shop, then indirect competition will come from men's clothing shops because they compete for the money families have to spend on clothes. However, that kind of competition probably won't mean much, as sales of men's clothing tends to be considerably less than sales of women's clothing, and fashion changes tend to be less important

Accountants who prepare tax returns for businesses face indirect competition from software companies who sell programs to prepare tax returns on your personal computer. In the past that kind of competition hasn't been important to accountants, but that may be changing. As more and more people become comfortable with computers, there is a greater possibility that they will buy tax software packages instead of visiting the accountant. Even though they haven't been important in the past, they could become a serious problem in the future.

## DIRECT COMPETITORS

Identifying your direct competitors means making a list of all the businesses in your market area that sell the same basic things as you do. Your market area is that geographic region where your customers live or the area in which competitors can affect your ability to draw customers. Let's say that you plan to open a garage doing mechanical and engine repairs and paint and body work. If you start this business in a small town, then you will probably expect people who live in the county to be your customers. You can expect to draw people from a radius of 20 or 30 miles, maybe even more in some areas. People who live farther away are more likely to find a garage closer to their homes when they need work done. So, identifying your competition means finding every garage in the county or every garage in that 30 mile radius of your business. You may be able to do this by looking in the yellow pages of the telephone book, but the best idea is to get out and look. Drive over your entire market area and look at your competitors. You're going to need to do this anyway to find out the best way to compete with them.

Let's say that you want to open a truck stop near the Interstate highway. You want to sell diesel fuel and gasoline and run a restaurant. You might even decide to have a motel adjoining the operation for truckers who need to rest overnight. What is your market area? Actually, since you are going to be relying on truckers stopping off the Expressway, your market area extends a long way up and down the highway. Truckers can be expected to drive an hour or two longer or stop an hour or two earlier to do business at a truck stop they like. That means that you will be in competition with all the truck stops located within 100 or 200 miles up and down the highway. If the Expressway crosses another Expressway in that distance, you need to look up and down the new highway as well. How do you find the competitors? Drive the highway and look.

It is crucial that you locate all the direct competitors in your market area because those businesses will affect your success. Even if you can look up the businesses in the yellow pages of the telephone book, you still need to go out and see them. Since these businesses sell the same basic things as you sell to the same people you will be selling to, you have to beat these businesses to win. Winning means getting more of the customers to come to your business rather than your competitors. How do you do that? Think about what you are going to offer that is better than your competitors provide. You also have to think about what they are offering that is better than you are providing.

Make a list of your competitors. Visit every one of them. Write down what you see as their strengths and weaknesses. Where are they located? Is it a good location? How good? Is it easy to find and easy to see? What are their prices? Their hours of operation? What about their product mix? Is it good? Do they offer any special services? What does the place look like? Is it clean and attractive? How about the people who work there? Are they friendly? Are they competent? What kind of advertising do they do? Do they have signs along the highway? How many? Are they lighted? Are the signs attractive? Do they have a lot of customers? Check at various times to see how well you think they're doing in terms of customers. You might want to recruit a few young people from the local area to park in various lots and count trucks and customers all day. The key is to learn what each competitor is doing to attract customers. How strong a competitor will each one be for your business? How can you beat each one? If you are careful in your investigation, you will find ways that you can beat each of the competitors in this process. It's a matter of seeing what each one is doing poorly and what each is doing well. It's a matter of seeing what each one is doing well and doing that thing better. It's a matter of seeing things you cannot do because you can't afford it, and specializing in things you can do. It's a process of finding out how to make your business better in some way than your competition.

## DISTINCTIVE COMPETENCIES

A *distinctive competency* is something that makes your business stand out from its competitors. It's the thing that you do best. It's the thing that makes you different and makes customers want to do business with you rather than with your competitors. Deciding what your distinctive competency will be is a process of identifying and understanding your competitors. It is an ongoing process. That means that you will need to keep checking out your competition in the future. You can't just check them once when you start. You have to keep informed about changes in who they are and changes in how they do business. How can you expect customers to prefer your business if you don't know why they should? You can't expect it to happen, you have to make it happen. That means that you have to consciously plan how to make your business different and keep it that way.

Your distinctive competency is especially important in a crowded market. In a community with which we are familiar, we watched a number of fast food restaurants open over a period of years. The community was quite small, but the first businesses seemed to be doing well. In fact, they did so well that they attracted additional businesses who set up next door or a short distance down the road. In three years, the number of fast food restaurants grew from three to six. In the fourth year, a new fast food business began construction. However, the number of competitors had grown to the point that they began to cut the market pie into pieces that were too small. Four of the existing restaurants had already cut back on the number of hours they were open and a new competitor was about the enter the market. Today, four of the businesses have closed, and the area is back to three restaurants. As the number of direct competitors grow, the potential market share for each business shrinks. In order to combat this situation, you need to ensure that you keep a strong distinctive competency. That's the only way to preserve your share of the market and ensure that it is your competitors who will suffer from the increased competition.

## INDIRECT COMPETITORS

Identifying your indirect competitors is very similar to finding the direct competitors. What is your market area? Which businesses in that market area will be in competition for your customers' dollars? Remember, indirect competitors don't sell the same things you do, they compete for the dollars that your customers have available to spend.

Let's say that you want to open a gift shop. You plan to offer unusual items that will make good souvenirs for tourists to buy as mementoes of their travel or as gifts for their friends and families back home. In the last section, we talked about how you would identify your direct competitors. It should be simple to locate all the gift shops in your market area. How about indirect competitors?

You will really be in competition with every business that appeals to tourists because tourists only have so much money they can spend during their vacations. That means that you will be in competition with the water slide, with the carnival, with the petting zoo, with all the entertainment businesses, as well as the gift shops. If the tourists spend more money on the entertainment businesses, they will have less money to spend for souvenirs. That will mean that all the gift shops, including yours, will have less business.

Here's another example. Let's say you want to open a hair styling salon. You know that everyone who does hair styling, coloring or treating is a direct competitor. What about indirect competitors? Those products which are sold in drug stores for do-it-yourself perms, styling, and coloring are your indirect competitors.

So you see, the process of identifying your indirect competitors means thinking about businesses where your customers might spend the money they would otherwise spend with you. You can't really compete with these businesses like you can the direct competitors. We talked about a distinctive competency to make yourself different from direct competitors. With indirect competitors the best you can do is to be aware of them and of the effect which they might have on businesses like yours.

If you are about to start your business, think about whether indirect competitors can be a problem for you. If they can, be sure to check the market area closely for such businesses. You might decide to locate in a different place to avoid some of the indirect competition.

If you're already in business, you need to monitor the indirect competitors. If there is a change in the number or size of such businesses, you may need to think about how you will be affected and make a plan to minimize that effect. In some cases it might be as easy as changing your product mix. A few years ago, toy stores were facing increasing competition from computer games. The toy stores started selling computer games. In other cases, you might be able to change your location. If your gift shop is being hurt by the entertainment businesses, you might locate in the middle of those businesses. You could put your gift shop right down beside the entertainment businesses and draw off some of their traffic. In other cases, you might have to be careful with pricing. In that hair salon, if your prices get too high for your customers, more of them will be likely to start using do-it-yourself products from the drugstore. In other cases, you might have to change what you're selling. If you're an accountant, you might put in bookkeeping or payroll or consulting services to make up for a decline in tax business coming from those computer software packages.

The good thing about indirect competition is that all of your direct competitors face the same competition that you do. That means that if you do a very good job of setting up a distinctive competency and maintaining it, increases in indirect competition should hurt your direct competitors more than it hurts you. So you see, the best way to handle indirect competition is to handle direct competition. The existence of indirect competition really means that it is that much more important to understand your direct competition and be effective in distinguishing your business.

## REVIEW

If you go into business, you will have competitors. There are two basic types of competitors: direct and indirect. Direct competitors carry the same basic items or provide the same basic services that you do. Indirect competitors are those who do not sell the same things, but they compete for the same dollars.

It is easy to identify direct competitors. Just make a list of all the businesses in your market area that sell the same products or services you sell. That probably means listing all the competitors in a 30 mile radius. Examine the strengths and weaknesses of your competitors and see if you can do a better job.

You will need a distinctive competency. This is something which makes your business stand out from its competitors. It can be something you do better, the way you operate, the location or hours of operation you choose, the kinds of customer service you provide, the kinds and varieties of inventory you stock, or almost anything you can think of that will make your business different.

Identifying indirect competitors is similar to the process of locating direct competitors except that your base is probably larger. Your customers only have so many dollars. If they choose to spend those dollars in some other business, they can't spend them in your business. That's why businesses that sell the same general kind of goods or services are indirect competitors: grocery stores and restaurants and produce markets and bakeries; movie theaters, bowling alleys, ball games, and amusement parks; clothing stores, department stores, and mail order catalog companies. Remember that all of your direct competitors face the same indirect competition as you do.

Observation of your competitors can teach you a lot about how to compete more effectively. Think about the strengths and weaknesses of each one. Compare each one to your business. Think about your distinctive competency. As your business develops and you try different things, watch your competitors. Do your actions affect them? If one of your competitors changes something, do you need to respond? Remember that if you can control the direct competition, you will also be controlling the indirect competition as well.

Starting and managing a successful business means understanding who your competitors are and how your business is affected by them. You must constantly monitor your competitors, and know what their strengths and weaknesses are. You must keep focused on a distinctive competency which makes your business different from your competitors and which makes more customers want to buy from you rather than your competitors.

## QUESTIONS, EXERCISES AND CASES

### Questions

1. What is the difference between direct and indirect competition?

2. Look at potential competitors of yours (or those you identify in your community, if you do not have nor plan to have a business). Indicate the direct and indirect competitors for that business.

3. Define the following terms:

   a. Competition
   b. Direct Competitors
   c. Indirect Competitors
   d. Market area
   e. Distinctive Competency

4. Identify the business you wish to start or one from your observation and indicate its distinctive competency.

5. Indicate whether your distinctive competency is sustainable. Why or why not?

### Exercise

1. Look at several small businesses in your town. Can you identify the distinctive competency? Do they have one? Can it be sustained for any period of time?

2. For the business you are thinking of starting, identify the direct and indirect competitors.

### Case

*My dojo will provide children with opportunities to develop discipline through intensive training in karate. Using the Japanese model of respect and self control, my students will participate three afternoons per week in karate lessons ranging from beginner level through the brown belt level. They will gain athleticism and health, as well as developing self confidence and learning self discipline.*

*My dojo will provide women with opportunities to develop self defense skills. Women will learn how to defend themselves from a variety of physical attacks and in the study of karate gain confidence in themselves while improving their health and well being.*

*My dojo will provide adults with opportunities to develop self confidence. My students will study Japanese style karate and develop skills in self defense while improving their physical conditioning and overall health. Ranging from the beginner level through the black belt level, my students will progress through the art to reach mastery of the discipline and a level of self confidence which cannot be obtained in ordinary physical fitness training.*

*Finally, my dojo will offer people battling weight problems and people in poor physical condition the opportunity to lose weight and improve their overall health. Through the use of weight training and the use of physical fitness machines and with the support of an individually prepared fitness training and dieting guide, my clients will be able to progress to any level of health, strength and weight loss which they might desire.*

So goes the vision statement prepared by Randy for his karate school after being in business for a while. The school seemed to be taking the town by storm. The sudden proliferation of movies dealing with the study of karate and the wider goals of self discipline and self confidence provided a ground swell of appeal to not only future karatekas but to the parents as well. Riding on this wave of sudden popularity, many schools sprang up. Many black belt students who had worked under other teachers suddenly decided to go out on their own. The needs were not great. A large empty building with mirrors would suffice. The Kar Ren Dojo opened its doors on just such a shoestring and began attracting students by the score.

The building had belonged to Randy's family and he was a second degree black belt. He had large numbers of students vying for his attention and no one was too young or too old to learn. Randy had a better rapport with the young kids than with his older students but soon the classes were so large that he had to break them apart in order to handle them. He handpicked several students for rapid promotion and began letting his senior students take on some of the responsibility for teaching the classes. The students were proud and a steady source of free labor.

The success of the studio was evidenced by the new Porsche Randy was driving and the expansion of the dojo into a weight and exercise facility. A new dojo was opened in the neighboring town, 20 miles away, as demands and dreams drove expansion.

There were presently 150 karate students paying $35.00 per month for three one hour lessons per week. The students were divided into beginner and advanced classes: one group for children under 16, and one group for adults. Thus, four classes per week were taught in each of the two facilities. Since all of the karatekas were students or employed elsewhere, all class took place after 3:30 PM. There were slightly more students in the older facility than in the newer one.

There were 15 weight students who worked out an average of five times per week. These students paid a membership fee of $25.00 per month. There were 5 students in the newer building and 10 in the original location.

1. Who might be Randy's direct competitors?
2. Who might be Randy's indirect competitors?
3. What do you think that Randy's turning over his teaching duties indicates?
4. From which element of the school are the most revenues generated?
5. From which element of the school are the more expenses incurred?
6. What do feel is his distinctive competency or does he have one? Explain your answer.

# CHAPTER SIX

## HUMAN MOTIVATION

### INTRODUCTION

To plan any kind of marketing campaign, you have to understand something about why people buy the things they do. The idea is that you are going to try to persuade people to buy what you're selling and to buy it from you, rather than one of your competitors. To be successful at marketing, we need to know something about human nature.

People buy things for complex and poorly understood reasons. The easiest way to think about those reasons is to look at the *'who, what, when, where, how and why'* of a person's decision to buy. The 'who' refers to the people who buy a product or service. When we identify the people who will be buying from us, we have identified the target market. A target market is a group of people to whom particular products or services are sold. It is one of the most important concepts in marketing because identifying the target market allows us to focus our marketing activities in the right place.

### BUYER CHARACTERISTICS

Very few things are attractive to everyone. That means that the people who buy a particular product or service can usually be classified by age, sex, education, occupation or profession, family income, social status, and a host of other factors. Understanding those factors make it easier to appeal to the appropriate group. Why do athletic shoe companies use professional athletes to promote their products? It is because they have done extensive research and they have found that most of their customers are middle and upper income people between 15 and 35, who like sports, and who are influenced by what athletes say and do. This does not mean that everyone who wears athletic shoes fits that description, nor does it mean that there is anything wrong with people who fit that description. It simply means that in the athletic shoe business, a large number of potential customers can be impressed and influenced by using professional athletes as sales people.

It doesn't matter what kind of business you start, one of the first things you have to do is identify the target market. If you plan to open a hardware store, you must know something about the kind of people who buy hardware. For many products, like hardware, there has been a great deal of research into target markets. This information is published and can be found in any large library. For example, we know that in the hardware business, the target market is male, middle income, 20 to 50, who own their own homes, who like hobbies, and who are into 'do-it-yourself' repairs. If you're going to open a hardware store, then the first thing you should do is find a location for the store in a community which has a large population of middle aged, homeowners and a number of successful stores which sell hobby and craft, and do-it-yourself supplies. Then you need to plan advertising and marketing efforts which will appeal to the target market. Discovering your target market is common sense, but it's easy to overlook obvious things in the excitement of starting a new business.

There is one more aspect of the 'who' issue which we need to discuss. The person who buys something is not necessarily the one who uses it. For example, most toys are used by children, but they are purchased by adults. That means that to be successful, a toy store has to offer toys which will appeal to children as well as their parents and grandparents. Marketing efforts need to be aimed at both groups. This will require different marketing approaches and messages. Saturday morning television is saturated with toy commercials aimed at children. These commercials concentrate on how much fun a toy is. Most parents and grandparents don't watch Saturday morning cartoons, so advertising aimed at them must be shown at other times: During the 6:00 news is always a good time. Then, the message is more about the safety and educational value of a toy rather than how much fun it is; or, it might be that the commercial talks about a toy that can keep a child quiet for a long time. Now that's a toy *any* parent would buy!

## THE UNDERLYING DEMAND

What people are actually buying may not be obvious. For example, think about a restaurant in a college town. In most college towns, there are lots of restaurants from which students may choose. What makes them select one restaurant frequently enough to make that business successful? Obviously, food is not the only factor. A location convenient to the students will clearly be a major factor, but is there anything else? What makes you choose a restaurant when you decide to go out? Would it make any difference to your decision if you knew that you would see other people who were friends at a particular place? What if you knew that you would be able to sit down and talk with your friends when you got there? If you plan to open a restaurant, it may well be that what you will be selling is entertainment as much or more than food. If so, then you will have to design a place where lots of people will feel comfortable and where they can come and meet their friends.

Consider a hamburger restaurant located on an expressway. Is it food that such a place sells or is it convenience? Does it make a difference? It certainly will. Speed of service will be more important to a restaurant selling to people who are in a hurry while food quality will be more important to a restaurant selling to people who want a taste treat.

The 'what' which a business sells must be clearly understood in order to sell effectively. If convenience, service, speed or other factors are more important than the merchandise, then that is what you must promote; what you must sell.

The issues are complicated by the fact that you can craft an approach to selling a product or service that appeals to an entirely different motivation. We used to use toothpaste to illustrate this concept. There are some toothpaste companies that sell based on tooth decay prevention, and other toothpaste companies that sell based on enhancing sex appeal with whiter teeth. Today, a much better illustration is "green" marketing. A number of stores, products and services are sold on the basis of environmental protection. If you think about it, a major part of the "what" motivation is based upon the entrepreneur's strategy and his or her decision about how to define a target market.

## TIMING ISSUES

One of the major problems which a restaurant faces is the fact that people like to eat at set times each day. That means that the restaurant must have enough tables to handle the load during those times and its kitchen must be able to keep up with the orders, but it will have too many tables, excess capacity, and unnecessary expense most of the time.

The timing issue is closely related to the target market of a business. For instance, if a business appeals primarily to middle income, working people, it must be open during the times those people have available for shopping. The issue of timing is even broader.

Most businesses have seasonal patterns. That means that they sell more of their products and services at certain times of the year than at other times. Consider a novelty and gift shop located in a vacation resort. Such businesses frequently close after the tourist season to save money because they know that the sales volume at other times of the year are too low to cover the cost of being open. Even when the seasonality is less drastic, it still has an effect and marketing activities need to be closely meshed with the seasonality factors of a business.

Timing the opening date of a new business cannot be accomplished without knowledge of the business' seasonality. One restaurant with which we were familiar started in a college town. It opened its doors in June after most of the students in town had gone home for the summer. The summer school population of the town was dramatically lower than at other times of the year, as is the case in most college towns. That restaurant lost so much money during its first summer of operations that it was never able to recover and it went out of business within six months.

Another aspect of the 'when' issue is the frequency, or how often people buy things. People buy soap more frequently than they buy cars. That means that you sell soap differently than you do cars. Soap is a consumable item. That means that it is used up frequently and you have to buy more. Cars are durable items. They are used up over a longer period of time and people don't buy them as often as they do soap. Many businesses selling consumables try to develop brand loyalty. They want customers to buy their products every time. Pepsi wants you to always buy a Pepsi instead of a Coke and so their marketing efforts are aimed at developing that loyalty. It is harder to develop brand loyalty in durables, so businesses selling those kinds of products try to convince customers that their products are superior in price or quality or performance. The same holds true for services.

Grocery stores want you to come back again and again. A real estate listing service knows you won't use them very often, so they have to have a different approach to marketing than the grocery store.

The frequency of consumption issue has huge ramifications. If your customers are tourists and you expect them to buy from you once during their vacations, then it is crucial that you choose an area with a large number of tourists arriving each week. A family restaurant might expect people to frequent the store twice each month, but an expensive, gourmet restaurant might be better advised to expect customers to frequent the store twice each year. Can you see the differences required in the market area to support the different concepts?

## LOCATION ISSUES

The issue of 'where' people buy is one of the reasons that shopping centers and malls are so popular. Stores like to group themselves in a location which is convenient to shoppers. In the 1950s, downtown areas were the most convenient available, so store owners grouped their businesses there. It's different now because of people living in suburbs and because of the change in their life styles. Now, a major social problem facing American cities is the decay of downtown shopping areas caused by the stores moving to malls and shopping centers.

Malls and shopping centers have more going for them than just convenience. The stores can piggyback on each other's customers. Small stores can take advantage of the large number of customers which a large store draws by locating near it in a mall. In addition, the location of so many stores in a mall tends to draw people because no matter what they are looking for, they are likely to be able to find it in the mall. The more people who are walking around in a mall, the more likely stores are to be able to sell them something.

This brings us to an important point. The rent in malls and shopping centers is generally higher than most other places. New business owners frequently think that they have to locate in a cheaper place to save money. That's not always wise. Generally, the higher rent means that the location is more desirable. In a mall, you won't have to spend as much money in marketing to draw people to your store. You can piggyback on the people being drawn by the other stores. That could make the more expensive location turn out to be cheaper in the long run.

Location is not as important for some kinds of businesses. If customers are not going to be coming to the business, then you don't have to worry about being convenient to them. Trucking companies worry about access to interstate highways and good roads. A manufacturing plant may have to worry about having space to expand.

Location may be crucial to some businesses. Banks are now locating in grocery stores or in malls. Many businesses locate in the middle of mall walkways. These operations are sometimes called kiosks and the key to their survival is the location.

The final point we want to make about location is that it can affect your image. The image is what people think about your business. Think about a young lawyer or accountant just starting a new practice. If that person hangs out a sign on an old converted house, it gives quite a different image to customers than if the sign were on the front of a new, modern office building.

We have yet to mention buying on line. That is such a critical and important point that we intend to devote a entire chapter to Internet selling, or e-marketing, as we will call it. For now, we will focus on physical answers to the "where" question.

The "what" and "where" questions interact with each other in a major way. One of the reasons that piggyback marketing works so well in a mall is that shopping has become a form of entertainment. That means that a large number of shoppers are not going to the mall to buy a particular product, they are going for entertainment, and they will buy items which appeal to them during their perusal of the mall. On the other hand, shopping convenience can be a major factor in a decision to shop at a large department store. Frugality could be a major factor in the attraction of a Walmart or KMart.

## PURCHASE FUNDING

If we asked you how people buy things, you might say, "why with money, of course", and laugh. But, if you think about it, people often do not use money. They frequently use credit cards. Sometimes they use lay away plans. Sometimes they borrow money. It is important to understand how people will buy the product or service which you intend to sell.

One client we worked with sold satellite dish antennae. The dishes ranged in price from $1,000 to $4,000. We asked the owner how people bought his antennae. He said that he required cash. He refused to consider any alternatives. As you might guess, new competitors began to spring up who started offering financing arrangements for their antennae. Our client's sales volume fell off, and he finally had to sell his business. Our client's failure to offer financing gave his competitors an advantage.

Many entrepreneurs hate credit cards, not just because they are a lot of trouble to handle, but because they also cost money. The credit card firms charge you a fee for allowing you to accept their cards. This fee may run from 2% to as high as 6% depending on the volume of business you have each year. Despite all the problems they create, in some kinds of businesses you will have to take credit or debit cards in order to stay in business. For example, a motel operation which does not take cards will find itself at a distinct disadvantage. The important point is that you need to know how people expect to be able to buy from you and you need to prepare to satisfy their expectations.

Today, it is increasingly the case that stores do not want to accept cash; or, at least, not checks. It is much easier to confirm financial viability with a credit card or debit card. Bad checks continue to plague us, and counterfeit bills still arise. In some nations, counterfeiting is a major issue.

If you will be selling to commercial clients, you may be forced to provide invoicing and accounts receivable financing. Commercial customers do not expect to have to pay for the goods and services which they buy. The purchasing and payment processes are separated, and the company expects to be billed, and to submit payment through its normal processes. The larger the customer, the slower these processes can be. It is entirely normal for a small business selling to a large client to have to wait 90 or even 120 days for payment. In this case, the "how" becomes a major factor, and you must be prepared to sustain that wait period.

## BUYER MOTIVATION

We've really been talking about why people buy things in this entire chapter because everything we've mentioned influences the decision; but everything we've talked about has been general in nature. That is, we've focused on the general factors which influence a group of people, the target market. If we think about an individual and we try to understand that person's motivation for buying a specific thing, the issue becomes much more complex.

We often talk about products and services as being necessities or luxuries, things people have to have to live, and things people like to have. Food is a necessity, but why does an individual shop at one grocery store rather than another? Why does a person buy one brand of bread rather than another? Jewelry and gift shops sell luxuries, but the same questions apply. The answers are not simple and we really don't understand the process very well. That's because an individual's choice is affected by psychological and sociological factors.

Different producers of the same product frequently have different marketing approaches. We mentioned toothpaste earlier. One toothpaste company advertises its product as the best in cavity prevention. Another toothpaste company talks about how its product whitens teeth and freshens breath. The first company believes that people buy its toothpaste because they want to protect their teeth. The second company believes that people buy its toothpaste to enhance their sex appeal. Both companies are successful, so both approaches work.

The differences in marketing by the toothpaste companies come about because there are two basic approaches to take in designing your marketing strategy. The first is to try to find out through market research what the primary motivations are for people to buy a product. Then you design the marketing to appeal to those motives. That's what the first toothpaste company has done. Its market research identified cavity prevention as a primary motive for people to buy toothpaste. The fact that it has been successful means that a large number of people do buy toothpaste to prevent cavities and the company has been able to convince many of them that its toothpaste is the best cavity fighter.

The second approach to designing a market strategy is to try to create a reason for people to want your product. That means that you use marketing efforts to create a demand rather than trying to tap a demand that already exists. That's what the second toothpaste company has done. It decided that it might be possible to make people think about toothpaste the same way they think about cosmetics, as a way to make themselves more attractive. The fact that it has been successful means that its approach worked. It has been able to persuade a large number of people that toothpaste can make them more attractive and that its toothpaste makes them look the best.

Understanding why people buy things is difficult. The two basic approaches which we can use are those in the toothpaste example. Like the first company, we can try to identify motivations by doing market research. This means that we ask a large number of people questions in a survey. We can mail surveys, we can call people on the phone, or we can stop them on the street or in the mall. We have to be very careful to try to identify the target market first, so that we don't ask the wrong people. We also have to be careful how we go about making up questions and collecting people's responses. It's easy to sway people by the way we handle questions so that we don't get their true feelings. Market research is a difficult process and entire books are written about how it's done.

The other approach is to do what the second toothpaste company did. We can think up a strategy which we think might work and try it. If it doesn't work, we can try something else. If we keep trying different things, we can learn more about the target market. As we learn more about them, we learn more about how to influence them. The second toothpaste company ran a variety of ads over the years and it kept careful records to see how they worked. Over the years, the company fine tuned its approach by changing its ads as it learned what worked better. The problem with this approach is that it takes time and can be expensive.

Understanding the *why* of the purchasing decision may be the single greatest requirement for growth of your venture. The key aspects of our understanding of this critical motivation are displayed in Table 1. As the table displays, we believe that the motivation varies with the level of basic need for a product or service. If your venture supplies a product or service which satisfies a basic need, we believe that your growth will be determined by how well your marketing approach conforms to the underlying purchase motivation. A major aspect of that success is based upon making people believe that your offerings are more personally or professionally appealing than that of your competitors. That's because there are always competitors for all the basic needs or requirements of people or businesses. If your venture provides products and services which do not fill basic needs and requirements, then you are less concerned about competition, as the table suggests, because alternative choices do not play the same role in the purchasing decision. Success based on impulse or whimsy involve timing, pricing, and a creative appeal. Success based on rationalization involves a more in-depth promotional approach because you are striving to support the development of that rationalization. This strategy is the responsible for much of the explosion of the so called *infomercials*. Ventures supplying these items are striving to move them from the caprices of impulse or whimsy to the category of a useful, practical and valuable commodity while avoiding the problems of competitive choice. When that approach is successful, the results can be tremendous.

**Table 1**
**Why People Buy**

**Products or Services Which Satisfy a Basic Need or Requirement**

People tend to buy these items when they discover or perceive a need for them, and they tend to select items which they know about or which they learn about, items which they can physically obtain without a perception of undue effort, items which they believe that they can afford, and items which they perceive as providing them the greatest level of personal or professional satisfaction when compared to alternative choices.

**Products or Services for Which There Is No Basic Need or Requirement**

People tend to buy these items on impulse, as a result of whimsy, or as a result of a rationalization of potential, future need, and they tend to purchase these items when they discover their existence, and when that discovery is supported by a perception that they can afford the purchase.

**Products or Services Which Embody Entertainment**

People tend to buy these items when they desire to be entertained, or when the process of purchasing the item is itself entertaining, and they tend to select items which they know about or which they learn about or which they discover, which they perceive as physically obtainable without undue effort, which they perceive as affordable, and which they perceive as more entertaining than immediately available alternative choices.

The entertainment category can encompass products or services in both of the other areas and television shopping networks have discovered that, as have a number of producers of infomercials. The sales process itself attracts people who may or may not realize that they are being entertained and the promotion draws the customer into the act of entertainment by providing a call-in opportunity to interact with the actors in the broadcast. Also, auctions embody entertainment into the sales process, and people will frequently find that they buy more things and pay more for them at an auction than they would have normally expected. The same is true for flea markets and road side shops selling fruit and vegetables, etc. The actual purchase decision may be based on impulse, whimsy, or rationalization, but it can also be based on a perception that the process of purchasing can itself extend, enlarge or enhance the entertainment.

If you are providing an entirely new product or service based on a new invention or a new process, then you still have to appeal to one of the basic categories of buyer motivation. Since your market does not know of the existence of your invention, you have to first support their discovery of your offering. How do you make that sale? We'll return to that question in a later section, but we need to extend our foundation with more background on marketing strategy.

## COMMERCIAL CLIENT MOTIVATION

A sale to a commercial client is actually made to an individual; that is, the purchasing decision made by a corporate customer is actually made by an individual or by a team of individuals. People are doing the buying, so to sell the corporate customer, we must sell the people. Their motivations and market responses are exactly the same as for consumers with one complication: the needs of the corporation, company or organization which they represent. We must craft our approach so that the people who make the purchase decision perceive that their own organization will benefit from the transaction. However, the most important part of the purchase decision is that the decision makers perceive that they are personally benefitting from the purchase.

Consider that corporate customers buy two types of products and services: those required to support the direct production of income; and, those which are not required to support the production of income. In the former category will fall raw materials used in a manufacturing process, machines and equipment used in production, materials and supplies used in the company, etc. A cross country trucking company requires trucks, trailers, oil, fuel, tires, repairs and maintenance, insurance, dispatching facilities, communication support, etc. It may require loading and unloading equipment, lifts, docks, pallets, pads, storage, parking, and the list continues. If you are selling any of these items, then your products or services will clearly be judged by the purchase decision makers on the basis of how well they will support the company. They will also be interested in the price, the speed and dependability of supply, and the ease of purchase and resupply. However, the purchase decision makers will also be interested in buying from a vendor who makes their individual lives and professional lives better. That is, buying from a vendor who saves the decision maker(s) time, effort and money, while making the decision maker(s) look wiser, quicker and more professional inside the company.

But, don't forget that there is a second category: those goods and services which are not required to support the production of income. These items provide lots of opportunities for entrepreneurs and small firms. A former student of ours provides management development services to large firms. His is a one person operation, and the services he provides are really far removed from the actual operations of any of his clients. He has been successful because he has succeeded in providing services in which the purchase decision makers are also the consumers and he provides these consumers with services which make the job of personnel management easier. His services also allow his clients to feel that their personnel decisions are made in a more independent and objective fashion. In other words, he makes the personal and professional lives of his clients better.

The key aspects of our understanding of the commercial purchase motivation are displayed in Table 2. As the table displays, we believe that the motivation varies with the two types of purchase decisions. In the case of what we might consider the basic needs, we believe that your growth will be determined by how well your marketing approach conforms to the underlying purchase motivation. A major aspect of that success is based upon making purchase decision makers believe that your offerings will support the company efficiently and effectively, but that you will provide a more personally and professionally satisfying purchase experience than that of your competitors. That's because there are always competitors for all the basic requirements of commercial ventures. If you provide products and services which do not fill basic needs for the commercial client, then you have much more opportunity to differentiate yourself by preparing an approach which demonstrates a greater level of personal and professional satisfaction for the purchase decision makers. You need to demonstrate a linkage or a rationalization which ties back to corporate performance, but the primary success factor will revolve around making the decision makers happier with you and your goods, and making yourself as unique as possible.

**Table 2**
**Why Commercial Clients Buy**

**Products or Services which Support the Production of Income**

Purchase decision makers tend to buy these items when they discover or perceive that the company has a need for them, and they tend to select items which they know about or which they learn about, items which they can physically obtain without a perception of undue effort, items which they believe that the company can afford, which they believe will satisfy the needs of the company efficiently and effectively, and items which they perceive as providing them the greatest level of personal and professional satisfaction when compared to alternative choices.

**Products or Services which do not Support the Production of Income**

Purchase decision makers tend to buy these items when they discover their existence, and they select items which they perceive that the company can afford and for which a corporate value can be inferred or rationalized, and they tend to select items which they perceive as providing them the greatest level of personal and professional satisfaction when compared to alternative choices.

Now that we know something about motivation, we can begin to think about a marketing strategy. For new businesses we need to learn how to penetrate the market and for existing businesses we need to learn to tap an existing market; thus marketing for startups is different from existing businesses and the approaches and strategies are different.

## REVIEW

To plan any type of marketing campaign, you must understand why people buy the things they do. This means understanding the who, what, when, where, how and why of marketing. The who of the buying decision is the target market. It includes both the people who use the product or service as well as those who buy the product or service for others to use.

What people buy may not be obvious. If convenience, service, speed or other factors are more important than the merchandise, then that is what you're selling. If the entertainment is more important than the food, then that is what you're selling. The important point is that you must promote and sell what people are actually buying.

When people buy depends to a large extent on timing. Seasonality is also an issue as well as the opening date and the frequency of purchase. Frequency of purchase varies between consumables and durables and dictates how important developing brand loyalty will be.

Location is emphasized by the where aspect of the buying decision. Not all sites are attractive to all businesses. You must choose the one which best fits your needs and image. In fact, this issue of image is crucial to business success and it embodies the total impression which people have of your business.

The obvious response to how people buy is money, but that can take other forms such as cash, credit cards, debit cards, layaway, loans, or accounts payable. It is vital to consider how people will expect to pay for your product or services and to make appropriate arrangement to be able to handle their expectations.

Understanding why people buy is difficult. We can identify motivations by doing market research, but the best approach is to experiment. Try different things and different marketing appeals and watch the response of the target market. Remember that marketing to a commercial client also takes planning. The better we understand the motivation of our target market, the better we can plan a marketing strategy.

## QUESTIONS, EXERCISES AND CASES

### Questions

1. Define the following terms:
   a. Target market
   b. Seasonality
   c. Consumables
   d. Durables
   e. Brand loyalty

2. Examine the who, what, when, where, how and why of purchasing a cellular phone? A Flat Screen TV? A Barbie Doll or GI Joe ? Pepsi or Coke? Tax Preparation Software?

3. Why is brand loyalty not as important a consideration in the durables industry? There are some cases in which brand loyalty may be considered. What are they and why?

4. Why is it important to be able to identify why people buy? What is involved in the *why*?

5. Explain the motivation in designing a strategy for a corporate client as opposed to a consumer client. Which is more difficult and why?

### Exercise

1. Notice several products and/or services in your neighborhood and see if you can ascertain why people buy that particular product or service. Are they using the best approach? Would you do something different? What if it were your business, what would you do?

**Case**

A marketing approach which was first used by a friend of ours is becoming much more popular. It was an approach that everyone said would not work, in a industry that had formalized its approach over decades. What is this, you might ask? An automobile dealership.

For decades cars have been sold by salespersons, typically male and hard chargers. Since these individuals are paid on commission, then from the dealership's perspective, they are considered free goods, since their commission dictates their pay check.

But our friend had a different idea. He decided to start using a posted price approach to his cars. That meant that whoever came on the lot would decide to purchase the car or not based upon the price in the windshield. There would be no negotiations, which might take all day or the better part of a day, and no stress on the part of the buyer.

What a new concept! Our friend was derided by all the dealers in the area as being crazy, but he proved them wrong. He was able to sell more vehicles annually than all of the others put together. How did this happen? Let's analyze:

1. Who is the target market? Who makes the purchase decision? Are they the same or different?
2. What is being purchased at this dealership beyond the vehicle?
3. When should the dealership be open and why?
4. Why does this approach work? Explain your answer.
5. What happens to the salesmen in this approach and to the bottom line?

# CHAPTER SEVEN

## SELLING STRATEGIES

### INTRODUCTION

The key to selling anything is a strategy. A strategy is a plan of action. It sets out the approach you are going to take to try to persuade people to buy your products or services. The strategy, which we will call the marketing strategy, is not just advertising. It has to start with the basic approach you will take to dealing with people: Not just any people. The people we will be interested in are those in the target market. Before you can decide how you're going to sell, you need to learn something about the target market. That's usually done through marketing research.

### MARKETING RESEARCH

Marketing research means learning something about the who, what, when, where, how and why of the target market which we discussed in the last chapter. One of the best places to find information about a target market is to look in the library and online. For almost every product or service, there will be magazines and journals which publish information about the kinds of people who buy that item. There is also a great deal of information about the industry. An industry is made up of all the companies which sell the same or competing products or services. There will also be information about business in general. All of this can be useful for anyone wishing to start a business venture.

With the help of a reference librarian, you can find magazines and journals which are written especially for people who work in particular industries. For example, *Restaurant Weekly* is only one of many magazines which is filled with articles about the restaurant business. Your library probably has many of these journals and can find more on the internet. Then, there will be general business publications like the *Wall Street Journal, Business Week, Fortune, Inc., Advertising Age, Venture* and others. These are a valuable source of information. In addition, there are many books which have been written about markets and industries. In short, the library is always the first place to start when you want to learn something about business.

Today, the Internet is supplanting the Library and it is closer and easier to search for most people. The problem is that there is so *much* data on the Internet, identifying and sorting out what you want can be challenging. It just takes time and patience. As you work, remember that you are saving all that time that you would have used in commuting to and from the library!

## MARKETING SURVEYS

When most people think of marketing research they think of **surveys**. Surveys are questionnaires which are used to find out information about what kinds of things people buy and why they buy it. They can be used in person, over the telephone, or through the mail. Surveys can be a problem for small businesses. They are expensive and time consuming. Besides, conducting a survey requires a strong knowledge about statistics. If the survey is not prepared, administered, and interpreted correctly, it can be misleading. It is really a complex process.

About the best that a prospective business owner can do is to conduct an inexpensive, 'rough and ready' survey. These are used to gain an understanding of one or two things about the people who will be our customers. We can simply stop people on the street and ask questions. As long as you are careful to ask questions in such a way that the listener is not led to an answer, this can be a useful source of information.

Other surveys you can do involve measuring or counting something of interest. For example, you might want to know how many people or how many cars pass a certain point in a day. That kind of thing can be learned by spending a day counting. You might want to learn how many people go to the mall and shop at a particular store. Just watching the door of that shop should give you the information. It will also allow you to count the number of people who go in, but don't come out with packages, and the number of people who bring packages back to the shop for return.

## FOOTWORK

One of the best and least expensive ways to conduct market research is **footwork**. Just going out there and looking. Few people actually do much footwork when planning to start a business. Maybe they overlook it because it is so obvious. At any rate, there is no substitute for going out to look for yourself.

You should visit the local chamber of commerce. They might have some information which will be useful. In addition, talking with the people will give you ideas and let you make contacts which will be useful. Talk with bankers in the area. They can tell you a lot about a market and how strong the competition will be. They will also be good contacts later on when you get the business going and need to borrow money. Talk with people in industry associations. Your library has a directory of such people in all kinds of businesses. Remember to look for salespeople. Few people have a better insight into a market than salespeople trying to make a living in the market. Talk to governmental assistance agencies. If there is an office of the Small Business Development Center or its international equivalent in your area, it would be a serious mistake not to discuss a business start up with them. Other assistance agencies which can help you include the Service Core of Retired Executives, Economic Development Centers, and various business development and assistance programs of state and federal agencies, all of which have international counterparts in other nations. You can generally find out how to contact these through the internet.

One final point about footwork deserves special mention. Your competition may well be the most valuable source of information you can find. Walk or drive through the area where you plan to do business. Look at the yellow pages in the phone book. Talk to as many businesses as you can. Many potential competitors may be prepared to meet with you and discuss their businesses. Others may be reluctant to talk to a potential competitor. In either case, you can learn a lot just by close observation. Notice how they go about attracting and handling customers. You may see practices which you will want to copy, mistakes being made or spot find weaknesses which you can exploit.

## SELLING STRATEGIES

From a simplistic view, there are really only three ways you can go about trying to sell something. We can call them *push, pull and piggyback.* Most marketing strategies represent one of these approaches or a combination of them. We might say that there is one other approach which can be taken: no marketing strategy at all. If a business owner does not prepare a marketing strategy, then that owner has chosen this last method whether he or she realizes it or not. It is possible to be successful without any marketing strategy, but only in rare situations. If the target market has a high demand for an item and there is little or no competition, a business might be successful. There aren't many markets like that. For many years professionals, such as physicians, dentists, attorneys, accountants, and the like, believed that they didn't have to do any marketing. In fact, many of the professional associations had rules which prevented their members from doing any serious marketing. Now professionals are coming to realize, as most business people have known for years, that marketing is a necessary process for a successful business.

## PUSH STRATEGIES

In **push marketing**, you try to *push* an item through the market. Think about a company in the wholesale business. Let's say that we start a business selling bottled water. We inherited a piece of land that has a really good spring on it and the water from that spring is pure and delicious. We decide that there ought to be a market for people who do not have good water and who would be willing to buy good water for drinking. We want to sell our water through grocery stores, because that's where people buy things like this. In order for us to be successful, we have to have people buy the water, so we are really dependent on the grocery store to do the selling for us. Our strategy will be to call on grocery store managers and try to convince them to stock our water. We know that the grocery store will only stock the water if they think they can make money selling it. They only have a limited amount of shelf space and they have to use it for the products which will make them the most money. So how do we convince them to buy our water?

Think about it from the store manager's viewpoint. If we just bring in a truck load of water, someone has to handle it, stock the shelves, price it, put up signs inside the store advertising it, and things like that. It costs the store to handle the water. As a good sales pitch, you can offer to handle the water. You can give the store a good discount so that the water will provide a good profit for the store. Then you can bring the water in, stock it on the shelves, put prices on the bottles, and put up signs inside the store. You can check the store every week and restock the shelves, and change the signs inside the store. In short, you can handle everything for the store manager, plus offer a good price so that the water will make money for the store.

This approach is called a push strategy because we are trying to persuade the store to stock the product. The idea is that if people come into the grocery store and see the product, they will want to buy it. We are trying to *push* the product through the market. A push strategy means that we focus our attention on an intermediary. That is, we aren't really trying to sell water to the people who are going to drink it. We are trying to sell the water to someone else who will be selling it to the people who are going to drink it.

A lot of products are sold this way. It can be a good strategy for a business because it does not take a lot of money for advertising. Of course, there are problems. People have to buy the water and drink it, or you will never be successful. That means that you will need something to make your water more attractive when it gets in the store. Maybe that attraction is price. Your water might be cheaper than any other. Maybe an attractive sign or display on the shelf attracts attention. Maybe it will be the shape or size or color of the bottle you use which becomes the focus. The point is that you can't ignore the customer who will be buying the product. You have to make them want it, but you also have to make the grocery store want to stock the water in the first place.

## PULL STRATEGIES

**Pull marketing** is the easiest strategy to understand because you are exposed to that kind of marketing all the time. Every time you turn on the TV you see hundreds of commercials. All of them are trying to make you want to buy some product or other. The idea is to make the customer want something, then that customer will go to a store and ask to buy it. The store will have to buy the product from you because the store's customers want it.

Let's say that you have an idea for a new computer game. You're a really good programmer and you have written a new game which you believe that lots of people will want to play. How do you sell it? You could use a push strategy like the water example and go to stores which sell computer games, but if you have enough money there is another way. You could advertise the game on television, the internet, and in magazines. You have to pick magazines which you think people who play games will read. The idea is to make people see the advertising and want to buy the game. If your advertising is successful, people will go to stores and ask for your game. All you have to do at that point is make sure the stores know how to contact you to buy the games. You could handle that through letters and announcements that you mail to all the stores that sell games. When customers come in asking for your game, the stores will call you so that they can meet their customer's demands.

The problem with this approach is that it is very expensive. Most small business can't afford the kind of money it takes to run a really successful advertising campaign; but it can be very successful. We call it *pull* marketing because you are trying to create a demand in the people who use the product so that they will pull your product through the stores.

A consequent problem associated with pull marketing is the creation of the demand for a product or service which you cannot fill. You must have enough products on hand or enough people to supply the services once the demand is created or you can find yourself at a disadvantage. If you create a demand which you cannot fill, you have given your competition the sale. Remember the difficulties which were created the first year that Colleco marketed the Cabbage Patch dolls and the Adam computer. The demand they created was huge, but their inventory and production capacity could not keep pace with that demand. When you create a demand which you can't fill, your business goes to the competition and you may not survive the deficiency. Colleco paid the price and had to file for bankruptcy protection.

## PIGGYBACK STRATEGIES

The third strategy we're going to talk about is **piggyback marketing**. Let's say that you want to open a motel. You've worked as a desk clerk for a motel and you think you understand how the business works and you would like to start your own. You know that the big motel chains have a lot of people who do research to decide where to build their motels. They look at traffic patterns and population figures, and spend a lot of money in deciding whether a motel will be successful before they build it. You can't afford to do that, but you can piggyback on their work. All you have to do is find a successful motel and build yours across the street from it. You can offer cheaper rates and advertise your place with billboards and signs. When people get ready to stop at the motel, some of them will see your signs and decide to stay at your place instead. You are *piggybacking* on the demand which your competitor has created.

You see this strategy in shopping malls and shopping centers. Let's say you want to open a dress shop. You are really good with a sewing machine and you have some dress designs which you think will sell if people can only see them. You can't afford to spend a lot of money in advertising and you can't afford to travel to a lot of dress shops all over the country trying to persuade them to stock your dresses, but you can find a store location in the mall next door to a big department store. You know that a lot of people will walk by your store on their way to the department store or while they are window shopping in the mall. You put your best designs in the window and you piggyback on the traffic which the other stores in the mall create.

It works with services, too. Let's say you decide that you want to open a beauty parlor. You are good at cutting and styling hair and you want to start your own business. A good strategy might be to rent a location next to a grocery store in a strip shopping center. That would mean that everyone who comes to the grocery store will have to walk past your place. They will remember it better and be more likely to use your services than if they had to make a special trip to some out of the way location.

Piggyback marketing is one of the best ways for a business to get started. It can be used for most products and services and it is cheap and effective.

## COMBINATION STRATEGIES

Most successful businesses use a combination of strategies. The water supplier might choose to do some advertising in addition to trying to sell the grocery store manager. The motel, the dress shop and the beauty parlor might also do some advertising rather than just depend on their locations. The idea is that you can do a little pushing, a little pulling and a little piggybacking if you just understand how they work.

## REVIEW

The key to selling is not just advertising. Marketing strategies need to be developed which will be effective for the business.

In order to develop marketing strategies, you must first be able to identify your target market. This is best accomplished through marketing research.

Marketing research may be the result of a trip to the library to find information about the industry and your particular market. Surveys may give you valuable information about your target market. The best and least expensive method for conducting market research is foot work.

Observations and questions about the area, banks, other businesses, assistance agencies, and the competition will give you an incredible amount of very real information about the area in which you plan to locate your business.

There are only four marketing strategies. Push marketing involves trying to persuade a store to stock your product. It means focusing your attention on the intermediary store rather than on the end user or consumer of the product.

Pull marketing is that method associated with advertising. It means creating a demand for the product or service in the minds of the consumers so that they will then ask stores and retailers to provide the product or service for them.

Piggyback marketing is the least expensive and involves positioning a product or service in close proximity to its competitors. This means letting the competition create the demand and then you benefit from the traffic which the competition attracts.

The fourth marketing strategy is to do nothing. This strategy almost always leads to failure.

Combination strategies are most common and probably the most effective because we reach more of our target market using multiple strategies.

## QUESTIONS, EXERCISES AND CASES

### Questions

1. List the three basic approaches to marketing and give an example of each.

2. Which approach to marketing is better for small businesses just getting started, which at the growth stage, which is least expensive and therefore often more desirable?

3. What could be the most valuable source of information from a marketing perspective and why?

4. Define the following terms:

   a. Surveys
   b. Push marketing
   c. Pull marketing
   d. Piggyback marketing
   e. Footwork

### Exercise

1. Think about the marketing research aspects that we have discussed. How would you approach the market? How would you conduct the research necessary to ascertain viability of a product or service?

### Case 1

Several years ago, two former students asked us to help them to decide whether or not to purchase a car wash. They had both been downsized from their jobs and with their severance packages were looking to purchase a business. A business broker had suggested the car wash in a nearby town as a possible venture for them.

We looked at the demographics of the town, the returns for such businesses and we parked across the street from the car wash on Saturday afternoon and counted cars. What do you suspect was the result of the investigation? What if it had been in your town, and you and a friend had sought the same information? Would you make the purchase? Why or why not?

**Case 2**

A potential investor was interested in purchasing a franchise which sold barbeque sauce. He was totally won over by the advertising approach. It was a play on the concept of "You are a redneck, if...." of Jeff Foxworthy. The appeal was fun and entertaining, but it had another aspect which was how to get the product in the stores.

1. What approach would this be and how would one go about it?

2. Create an advertising campaign for the barbeque sauce using the "Redneck" motif.

**Case 3**

A friend was interested in selling a new brand of cigarettes. He had some experience as he had once owned a discount cigarette store and had heard of them. He truly thought that they had some potential, but he wasn't sure how to go about selling them. He could afford to purchase the rights to distribute them, but was at a loss as to what was involved in selling them through traditional channels.

1. What approach should he take?

2. What might it involve?

# CHAPTER EIGHT

# PRICING STRATEGIES

## INTRODUCTION

Now that you've decided that you're going into business for yourself, and you have some idea about what you're going to sell and how you're going to sell it, we need to think about how much you're going to charge for it. How do you decide that? Most people think that cost is the most important part of the price. That is, that you set the price by taking your cost and adding something to it for a profit margin. That's not entirely true.

You may have heard it said that price is a function of supply and demand. The supply part of that statement means that the less there is of an item, the more it is worth and conversely, the more there is of an item, the less it is worth. The demand side of that statement means that the more people there are who want an item, the more it is worth and the fewer people there are who want an item, the less it is worth. From a broad sense that statement is true; however, it doesn't do a business owner much good, because it's talking about the aggregate supply and demand. Aggregate means that economists are looking at all of the people in the entire country who want an item, and they are also looking at all of the items being produced in the country. We need more practical information. We need to know something about setting a price for our market area. What can we sell our product or service for in the area we will be selling in and what will be the reaction of our target market to that price?

Before we talk about setting that price, think about how important price will be to your business. Many people think that the best thing you can do is be as cheap as you can. That is *not* usually a good idea.

## PRICE DETERMINATION

The most important factors in setting a price are demand and competition. Competition means what other firms in the market area are charging for the same or similar item. Demand means how many people in the area want the item you're selling. It's really a matter of common sense. A buyer is only interested in acquiring something he or she wants at a price with which he or she is comfortable. The interest part is demand. The buyer must first desire the item or there will be no purchase. The second part is price. The only basis a buyer has for judging prices is the price charged for similar items by competing firms. So demand and competition are the main ingredients in setting price.

Demand can be a difficult concept. The demand for an item can include more than just the item itself. Demand can include such things as entertainment. A customer can be as interested in shopping for an item as in owning the item because shopping is fun. Many restaurants, especially those catering to young adults, sell more than just food. They are selling entertainment in the form of opportunities to meet and mingle with friends. Stores selling women's clothing may be selling the opportunity to model clothes as well as the clothes themselves, because many women like trying on different outfits. Demand can include things like convenience, both in location and hours of operation, service, advice and counseling, and a host of other factors which can be far afield from the item being sold.

The important thing to remember is that you may well be selling something more than the item which people take home with them. You must recognize that in making your pricing decisions and you must also be aware of it in managing your business. Customers are only happy when they get what they want at prices they think are fair. What they want may well be more than the obvious, so you have to make sure they get it.

As for pricing, that can also be a problem. There are three basic approaches which you can take to setting your prices. Your prices can be less than the competition, more than the competition, or the same as the competition. There are pros and cons for each strategy.

## PRICING ABOVE THE MARKET

If you want to set your prices higher than your competition, then you must be known for providing something which makes that price justifiable. For example, you might be known for a high level of quality and service. That would allow you to appeal to a target market which has a demand for high quality and service and is willing to pay to get them. For example, if you wanted to start a men's clothing store which charged high prices, then you would locate in an expensive area, such as a mall, and you would spend a great deal of money on store decor and amenities, to make the place look very nice. Then you would carry brand name clothes which had a reputation for high quality. You would have to employ sales people who were well dressed and courteous. You would need a large number of sales people to ensure that a customer never lacked for assistance while shopping. Sales people would be trained to remember customers' names and to call them by name. You might also offer services like store charge accounts and private sales for your best customers. In short, you want to appeal to a target market who demands special treatment and high quality and is willing to pay for it. That means that for your store to be successful, there has to be a large enough market in your area with those demands. An exclusive men's store could not be successful in a small town with a low to middle income level. It might very well be successful in a large city that has a large population of people at every income level, or in a small town with a high income level. The key point is that a firm which intends to pursue a pricing strategy of higher than the competition must make sure that sufficient demand exists in the target area to support the firm.

The second challenge is to make sure that all aspects of the operation are coordinated. You have to create an image of your store in your customers' minds and that image has to be consistent with higher prices. If you have a nice location, an attractive store, a high level of service, but you don't charge higher prices, customers will not believe that the merchandise is high quality. They may think you're selling 'factory seconds,' items which have not passed the quality control inspections at the manufacturer. In that case, charging low prices will *not* attract customers.

## PRICING BELOW THE MARKET

Pricing below the market refers to a strategy of offering prices below those offered by your competition. We're not talking about a sale or a discount plan. We're talking about a business which tries to always be cheaper than its competitors. If you choose this strategy, you're basically saying that you're going to compete on the basis of price. This can be a successful strategy if there is plenty of demand for what you're selling. You must remember that a lower price means less profit, so you have to sell more in order to have the same level of income. That means you need a large number of people in the target market.

A low price is an especially good idea if you're selling a commodity. A commodity is any product or service which is basically the same no matter who sells it. In this situation, the basic difference between competitors is price. Lots of items can be commodities; for example, food, especially meat and produce, lumber, hardware and home repair items, automobile accessories and repair parts, and services like plumbing, appliance repair and household maintenance. Just about anything can be a commodity except items which have a major brand image.

Soft drinks are good examples of the contrast between a brand image and a commodity item. In the grocery store you can see soft drinks which have a brand image, like Pepsi and Coke, and right beside them soft drinks which are sold as commodities. Pepsi and Coke spend a great deal of money in advertising to keep up the brand image of their products. The commodity soft drinks are not advertised at all. They just have much lower prices.

If you decide on a strategy of below market prices, you must be sure to coordinate that strategy with all other aspects of the operation. It's that image problem again. Customers will simply refuse to believe that low prices are being offered in plush surroundings. It's one of the reasons why it's hard to run a low price store in a mall. People generally expect malls to be more expensive so it's hard to convince them that any store in a mall has low prices.

The same is true for low priced services. People are not likely to perceive your services as being lower in price if you attempt to deliver them through an office or a venue which is exclusive appearing in nature.

## PRICING AT THE MARKET LEVEL

The most frequently observed practice among businesses is pricing at market levels. Marketers call this strategy **Follow-the-Leader** pricing. If you decide to use this strategy, you will try to price your goods and services at or near the prices which your competitors charge. The idea is to remove price from the purchase decision. You want to compete on some other basis, such as service, convenience, quality, or anything other than price. In other words, you are going to take the middle road between the above and below market pricing strategies which we have discussed so far.

Pricing at the market has several advantages over the other two approaches. Profit margins can be attractive. Such a firm is neither plagued with the low profits of a below market firm or the high costs of an above market firm. There can be less risk because people expect less from your business. That is, they don't expect you to have the lowest prices in town or to offer the highest quality in town. Since people expect less of you, it's easier to satisfy them.

## PRICE COMPETITION

Regardless of the pricing strategy you choose, you must keep in touch with what your competitors are charging. Obviously, you could not keep your prices in line with your strategy if you didn't know what your competitors were doing. Prices do change over time, sometimes rapidly, and you will have to keep pace with the changes. You will have to spend time monitoring your competitors. That means going to their businesses, checking their prices, watching how they do business, and thinking about how they compare to your operation. Of course, that's a good idea anyway because you will learn more than just pricing information and that will help you in running your business.

We need to make another point about price. It is a relative concept. That means that a firm can have a 300% markup, charge three times what it costs them for an item, and still be perceived as having low prices. Many items of jewelry fall into that category. A firm can also have a 10% markup, charge 10% more than their costs, and be perceived as having high prices. Many grocery items fall into that category. Customers do not know your costs. They make their evaluations based on prices at similar firms for similar items. That means that competition determines what is a high or a low price.

The really important aspect of the pricing decision is to ensure that it is consistent with the image of the business as established by the rest of the operations. In order for that to happen, a firm must consciously decide what its image will be, and what its prices will be, *simultaneously*. Nothing is more important and they are interactive because one of the most powerful contributors to the image of a venture is its pricing strategy.

Consider that quality is a difficult concept to judge, and few consumers have the knowledge or ability to actually determine performance quality of most of the goods and services which they buy. For example, just how long should a computer run before its hard drive or its screen fails? Most of us don't have an answer to that question, although we know that we are upset no matter when a computer fails; especially if we have not been backing up our data! This difficulty means that one of our primary indicators of quality is price. We tend to think of things that are more expensive as being of higher quality. Before you criticize that perspective, just remember that perception is reality. It does not matter what is; it matters what people believe!

## BUSINESS IMAGE

Nothing is more important to the success of a business venture than the **image** which it will portray to its customers. The business image is the way in which customers perceive the business; the thing that makes a business distinct from its competition; the thing a customer thinks of when seeing or patronizing a business. It is the personality of a business. You should think long and hard about how you want your customers to perceive your business. What do you want them to think of when they think of your business? What do you want them to think of when they see your business? You want to be distinct from your competition. What do you intend to do to make your business distinctive? You want your business to be as unique as your own personality makes you. What do you wish your business' personality to be?

Whatever image you decide to portray, you must be consistent with everything else involved in the business. You cannot send conflicting signals to your customers. We talked about this problem with the various pricing strategies. Price is an important part of the image which your business will have; but, it's not the only thing. In fact, the image of your business is affected by everything. From your location, to the appearance inside and out, to the sign out front, to the way inventory is displayed, to the way your people dress and talk, to the way customers are waited on, to the hours you are open, to the businesses that surround you, to the way your advertising looks, to your prices; everything affects your image.

If you have a negative image or a poorly developed image in the minds of your customers, you will be at a major disadvantage. In the case of a negative image, people will avoid buying from you if they can. A negative image means that customers are not comfortable in your business. It is only natural in such a case for people to avoid you. Yet, a poorly developed image will hurt you as well. It's like a person who has no personality. That person will have few friends. A business with no personality will have few customers. People will just forget your business is there when they go to buy. They will overlook you, fail to notice you, or just not think about you.

The point to remember is that you need to plan your image and make sure that everything is consistent with that plan, and that it stays consistent over time. If you're going to run a restaurant which is a meeting and greeting place for young people, then your location, hours, prices, menu, and decor need to be consistent with what young people like. More than that, your wait staff has to be friendly and courteous to young people. Your restaurant is going to be noisy. You can't go around asking people to keep it quiet and expect them to come back. On the other hand, if you're going to have an expensive restaurant which offers fine dining, you must keep people from becoming too noisy. You can't be all things to all people. So, you have to know what it is you want to be, and work hard to keep that image.

## REVIEW

Pricing is more than merely adding a percentage for profit to the cost. Understanding supply and demand is important, but far more important is understanding your target market and how it responds to price.

The most important factors in setting a price are demand and competition. Interest in a product or service creates the demand and how much the competition is currently charging must be considered in setting prices. Demand may well be more difficult to identify because the interest may be in intangible aspects of the business rather than the product or service itself.

There are three basic approaches to setting prices. Pricing above the market implies value added to the product or service so that higher prices are acceptable. Pricing below the market can be successful if there is sufficient demand for the product or service. Below the market pricing is especially appropriate for commodities.

Pricing at the market is the most frequently observed practice in business. Prices similar to those of your competitors provide attractive profit margins with less risk and allow your business to compete on something other than price.

Regardless of the pricing strategy you choose, a continual monitoring of the competition is mandatory so that you can keep your prices in the range which you planned.

The business image may be the most important consideration for your business because it permeates all the decisions which you must make: pricing, location, appearance, inventory, employees, hours, etc. A negative image is almost impossible to reverse, so it is tremendously important that the image be constantly monitored.

## QUESTIONS, EXERCISES AND CASES

### Questions

1. Why does competition determines what is a high or a low price? Explain your answer.

2. What are the factors affecting the purchase decision? Explain each of them.

3. What are the main inputs to price and why?

4. What is the purpose of price?

5. Define the following terms:

   a. Price
   b. Fair price
   c. Demand
   d. Market price
   e. Market
   f. Pricing at market
   g. Pricing over the market
   h. Pricing below the market
   i. Factory seconds
   j. Commodity
   k. Follow the leader
   l. Product/service advertising

6. What are the three methods for pricing?

7. Why do you not have a choice in your pricing decision unless you have a unique product or service?

8. Comment upon the following statement: Vision and image must match the demand of the market. Give an example of several venture in which there is a congruence of vision, image and demand and one in which there is a clash between those concepts.

9. Why do most ventures price at the market?

10. Why is it unwise to price below the market as a new venture as a competitive advantage against large, more established companies?

11. What additional elements are required to price above the market?

**Exercise**

1. Observe several businesses in your area and determine which pricing technique they are using. Do you think that what they are doing is appropriate to their business? Why or why not?

## Case

The business was a small gift shop located in a rather expensive section of suburban Atlanta. The owner, a lady in her mid forties, had called us in because she was losing money steadily and was at a loss as to the basis for the problem. The shop was beautiful. It had been in business for less than six months and was located in a shopping center with a good anchor store and excellent traffic patterns. The shop was tastefully decorated and the inventory was artfully displayed. There were plenty of indirect competitors, but no direct competitors within 10 or 15 miles of the shop. When we walked in, we were really impressed. The outside of the shop, its sign, and the shopping center in general were attractive and it was clear that there was an adequate population base to make the store successful.

At first we asked to look at advertising records and mockups, but the program looked fine, so we looked at the accounting records. One thing was puzzling; the gross profit margin had been stable at 20%. We thought that was a bit low for a gift and novelty shop, so we asked about markup policy. The owner said the policy was a 25% markup based on selling price, but occasional sales held the margin down a bit. Then we looked more closely at the inventory in the store and the prices.

We couldn't believe the bargains! The items were beautiful, including many glass pieces and art objects at prices which were well below the prices you would expect in Atlanta.

1. What advice should be given to the client?

2. What do you think her reaction would be?

3. What do you believe was the outcome?

4. What does this suggest about pricing strategy?

5. Which method is she pursuing and which method should she pursue?

# CHAPTER NINE

## IDENTIFYING COSTS

### INTRODUCTION

We all understand that you are planning to go into business to make money, but, what does making money mean? It means that your income from your selling activity is greater than your outlay for the costs of running the business. We call the income from your selling activity, revenue, and we call the outlay for your costs, expenses. If the expenses are greater than the revenues, you will lose money and you won't be able to stay in business very long if that situation continues. That means that an important part of the planning for any new business involves estimating your costs so that you can see whether the business can be successful. Let's define some terms.

All of the income which your business produces is called revenue. If you sell things, the money you get is sometimes called sales, but if you sell services, the money you get is usually called fees. That's why we simplify the process by calling all of your income, *revenue*, whether it comes from selling products or from fees you charge for services. We need to talk in more depth about the costs you will have.

### FIXED AND VARIABLE COSTS

We call all of the outlays of your business, expenses or costs. These are things like rent, the telephone bill, salaries to employees, insurance premiums, the cost of products you sell, or any other payment you have to make to keep the business going. The important thing about expenses is how they behave over time. Some expenses stay the same, or change very little, from month to month. Things like the rent or insurance premiums are like that. We call such expenses, fixed costs. Other expenses change a great deal from month to month. The cost for products you sell will go up if you sell more or go down if you sell less. We call such expenses variable costs.

The labels, fixed and variable costs, cause some problems because the names seem to say that the cost does not change at all or that the cost changes all the time. The key is whether an expense is directly related to revenues. Let's say you want to start a hair cutting and styling salon. If you start out with no employees, then all of your expenses will be fixed. You will have to pay rent, insurance, electricity, water, and telephone bills. You might lease your equipment or you might borrow money to buy it. If you lease it, that will be an expense, and if you buy it, you might have loan payments to make. The important point is that all of these costs will be the same whether you cut hair for 50 people or for 75 people. That's why we call them fixed costs. It doesn't matter that the telephone bill will not be exactly the same every month, or that the rent might go up after the first year. The fixed costs will not vary with the number of customers you have. Of course, that is only true within reason. If you have 500 customers next week instead of 50, you'll have to hire some people to help you cut hair and the cost will change. That's OK, the important point about the fixed cost is that they will not respond *immediately* to small changes in your sales activity.

Let's say you start a business to sell screen printed tee shirts. You will have the same kind of expenses as the hair salon, but you will also have to buy tee shirts. The cost of the tee shirts will change as sales change. If you print and sell 50 shirts, the cost for the shirts will be less than if you print and sell 75 shirts. We call the cost for the shirts, a variable cost. The difference is that variable costs respond *immediately* to any change in your sales activity, no matter how small that change might be.

Not every business will have variable costs. Think about the hair salon. The only way that a hair salon would have variable costs would be if the business employed several people and paid them a commission for their work. If each employee got a percentage of the price for each haircut or styling job, that cost would go up and down immediately as the sales changed. On the other hand, if the employees were paid a salary, that cost would not vary as the sales changed. If the business grew, you might hire more people, but small changes in sales activity would not affect the amount you pay them. This could even be true if you paid the people by the hour. If you had two employees and paid them by the hour, but they always worked 40 hours per week, that cost would not vary. It would be a fixed cost. On the other hand, if you have hourly paid employees and you send them home when there is no work to do, or call them in to work when extra customers show up, that cost would be a variable cost. In that case, more customers would mean more employees and fewer customers would mean fewer employees.

## COST PREDICTION

You can't make money until you can cover your costs. We call the difference between revenues and expenses, profits, but only if the revenues are greater than the expenses. If they are just equal, we say you are breaking even and it is this break even point that we want to think about in trying to decide whether your business will be feasible. In other words, how many customers do you have to get in order to break even? How many customers do you need to make a profit? It's a major part of deciding whether a business can be successful. Knowing your costs is also important in talking about the prices you will charge. And, of course, your prices can have an impact on your break even point, as well.

There is another reason to be concerned about costs. If you don't understand the costs of being in the business you plan to start, you can't predict what they will be and you can't control them. It's really not hard to understand costs. You just need to think about the costs from the view point of how your business will work. How will your business operate? What kinds of things will you do in this business? What kinds of expenses will those things cause?

A lot of things are common to all kinds of businesses. First, you must have a place for the business. Maybe you need a store or a shop, a warehouse or an office. You may need a sign out front and you may have to do a lot of work inside the place. You will have to have lights, power, water, telephone, heat, things we call utilities. You may or may not need employees. That will depend on whether you intend to do all the work yourself. You may need professional advice from an accountant or an attorney. You will probably end up hiring an accountant to handle your sales taxes, payroll taxes and income taxes. This will usually be a flat fee each month. Visit some accountants and talk to them about it. Find out what fees they will charge. You may need to buy a computer and some software. Will you need a cash register? If you are selling a product, you will have to buy the products. If you are selling a service, you may need supplies to support your work. A janitorial service needs cleaning supplies. No matter what you're doing, you will probably have to have insurance. You'll need insurance to protect your business and you may need insurance to protect yourself if you get sued. Maybe you will need some equipment. Restaurants need kitchen equipment. Maybe you will need furniture like desks and chairs, or maybe you will need display racks and cabinets, things we call fixtures.

Get out and look at businesses like the one you want to start. Look at what the business owns, where it is located and how it is operated. Make a list of everything you think you will need and start trying to find places where you can get the things you will need. Ask the people in the businesses you examine where they got the things you will need. The best thing to do is to get a job working in a business like the one you want to start. That way you will learn a great deal about running the business as well as about the kinds of costs it will have. When you're ready to go, you have to start with the physical layout of the business. Let's walk through an example of how it works.

## THE LAYOUT

Let's say that you want to start a restaurant. You're going to serve sandwiches and hamburgers for lunch and dinner, but you're also going to have specials like steak and seafood for dinner. You're going to do the cooking and you're going to hire people to do everything else. You think you'd like to be able to handle 30 or 40 people in your restaurant. How much will your costs be?

First, you need a place. You need to have an area in mind, then you can call real estate agents. How much space will you need? That's going to be the first question a real estate agent asks. How much do you need? Think about how you will set up the tables and chairs in your dining room. Are you going to use round tables? Square tables? Tables for 4 people or tables for 6 people? Big tables or little tables? Booths? Remember the image we talked about previously? What kind of image do you want this business to have? Let's say you decide you want a homey image and you decide to go with booths and small, square tables. Both the booths and the tables will seat 4 people. We go look at some booths and tables in a restaurant and we measure off how much space they take up. We decide the tables can be 2 feet square, but with people sitting at them, they take up a space 4 feet by 4 feet. People have to be able to walk around and between the tables and waiters and waitresses have to be able to serve the people. If we add 3 feet of walking around room between tables, we see that we will need a space 5.5 feet square for each table. That means that each table will need about 30 square feet. Now, the booths are about the same size as the tables, 4 feet by 4 feet, but they don't need as much room for people to walk around them. In booths, there is only one open side so we can get a lot more in a smaller space than we can tables. If we add a 3 foot wide aisle between rows of booths, then each booth will take up a space 4 feet by 5.5 feet. That's an area of 22 square feet.

Now we have a good idea of how much room we will need to handle a seating capacity of 30 or 40 people. Let's say we decide on 40 people. We know that we can put 4 at each table and at each booth. That means that we need a combination of 10 tables and booths. Draw it out on a sheet of graph paper. Keep the scale in mind and see how the tables and booths will fit together. If you're going to put in a salad bar, think about how much room you will need for it and draw it in your layout. Will you need room for a cash register? How much? How about the kitchen? How much room will you need for the stove, grill, oven, refrigerator, freezer, and dishwasher? How much room do you need for people to be able to work around each other? Where are you going to keep the clean dishes? How much room will they take up? Don’t forget the restrooms. Put all this in your diagram and lay out all of the work space.

Can you see how this process will let you decide on the space you need for your business? We might decide to use 6 booths with 3 along each side of the wall and 4 tables in the middle, two by two. Adding a salad bar at one end could take up the other wall and the cash register could stand at the front. This would take up a room 22 feet square, or 484 square feet. The kitchen and storage areas might need the same amount of space. If so, you know that you need a space of just under 1,000 square feet. Real estate agents can readily tell you about spaces they have for rent which have that much space and what your rent will be in various locations in the area. They can also tell you what the utilities are likely to run; the heat, lights and water. You can go out, look at some of the locations, check out the surrounding area and think about which one would be best for your business. Be sure that the location will fit the image you want your business to project. The agent will tell you about the lease you will have to sign for each location and you can begin to get an idea of which locations are more desirable. In each location, ask yourself several questions.

"Will people come to this place to buy from me?"

"Can they find me easily?"

"Can people get in and out easily and have room to park?"

"Will my customers feel comfortable here?"

"If the business takes off, will I have room to expand?"

"If the business doesn't do well, can I get out of the lease?"

You can do this same kind of layout for almost any business. If you're going to start a sporting goods store, a visit to several stores will help you figure out how merchandise is displayed and how much room it requires. You can use your layout chart to set up racks and displays for the various types of sporting goods you will be selling. Using your graph paper, you can determine the size of the space you will need.

## EQUIPMENT

There are businesses who supply special equipment. They can help you with equipment just like real estate agents can help you with a building. If you live in a city, you can probably look in the yellow pages of the telephone book and find businesses which sell restaurant equipment. In a smaller town, you may have to check in a nearby city. People who are already in businesses like the one you plan to start can help you locate suppliers.

Restaurant suppliers can sell you or lease you all of the equipment you will need. They can help you identify the kinds of equipment you need and tell you what it will cost. They can point you to people who make loans to buy the equipment or help you get a lease on the equipment. In either case, you will get a good idea of what it will cost to buy or rent the equipment.

There are suppliers for the equipment for most any kind of business you might start. From display racks to cash registers, anything you need can be bought or leased. The suppliers can tell you how much it will cost, tell you about loans to help you buy the equipment, or leases to help you rent the equipment.

## LEASEHOLD IMPROVEMENTS

If you have to make repairs to a building, build in counters or walls, take out walls, put in carpet, or do anything to get the building ready for your business, these are called leasehold improvements. If you make any improvements to the building, remember that they will belong to your landlord, the person who owns the building. That goes for anything you do to the building. The landlord may be willing to give you an allowance on your rent for leasehold improvements. On the other hand, the landlord may not be willing to let you make some types of changes to the building.

When you look at a place, visualize what you want it to look like. You want its appearance to match the image you have for your business. Make notes about changes you would like made. Call some building contractors and ask them to look at the place and tell you what it would cost to make the changes you want to make.

Be sure to remember the sign. Almost every business needs a sign outside. Think about what you want your sign to look like and where you want it to go. It must be highly visible and easily read. Most importantly, the sign must fit the image you have for your business. You may be able to rent one of those signs mounted on a trailer with flashing lights and set it up on the road outside, but will that fit your image? A sign like that might be very visible, but it could give people the idea that yours is a cheap place. Visualize what you would like to see in a sign. Sketch out what you would want it to look like. Then, call a sign company. Show them your ideas and ask about prices.

## SPECIFIC LOCATIONS

Rather than laying out your business and then looking for a location that fits your needs, you may want to do it in reverse. Let's say that you find a location that you really want. You think it would be ideal for the business you want to start. In that case, you have to make your business fit the space available. It's really easier than working from scratch because you can lay out the dimensions of the space on your graph paper. Now, it's just a matter of seeing if your business can fit into the space available.

There is one dangerous aspect of choosing the location first. People have a tendency to think that it's easier to rent a building that had a restaurant set up in it, rather than to start a restaurant where one has never been. They see an empty convenience store and think about renting it to start another convenience store. It is true that it's cheaper to start a restaurant in a building set up for that purpose. You frequently can get the equipment and furniture as well as the building. However, if you start a new restaurant where one has failed, you might be inheriting an image problem.

It may be that the location you pick out is the absolutely best place for your business, but that's not guaranteed to be true. Have you ever noticed a location where one business after another has started and failed? In our town, there is a small building in an excellent location for a restaurant just across the street from the University campus. The building is equipped with a kitchen and has tables and booths and everything needed to run a restaurant. It is highly visible, has good parking, good access, and is in walking distance of the dorms. In the last ten years, six different people have rented it, set up a restaurant, and gone into business. All of them failed within a few months of starting. One was a sandwich shop, one was a pizzeria, one was a family style restaurant, one was a hamburger shop, one was a delicatessen, and one was a Mexican restaurant. Each time, the new owners put up a new sign. Two of them painted the building. After the first couple of failures, people in town used to speculate about how long each new proprietor would last. By trying to save money, the people who started those restaurants fell into a terrible trap. They inherited an image of failure. Each failure made people in the community less likely to give the new business a chance. Those restaurant owners would have been much better off to spend a little more and get a location with no memories attached to it.

You run a risk anytime you start a new business in a location where a business just like yours used to operate. People are likely to connect your business in their minds with the business that used to occupy the building. Since the first business is now gone, this confusion of image is not a good thing.

## SALARIES AND WAGES

The next cost we need to think about is the cost of people who will work in the business. It's not hard to think about how many people you will need in your business. How many hours will you be open? How many people will you need during those times? How much will you have to pay them? Visit as many businesses like the one you want to start as you can. The process will be easier if you've been able to work in a similar business for a while. This will not only help you to understand the number of people you will need and how much you will have to pay them, it will help you with every part of starting your own business. Even if it is only a part time job, you will still learn a tremendous amount about running the business.

Think about that 40 seat restaurant we were talking about. Let's say you decided that you would serve lunch and dinner seven days each week. That's opening at 11:00 AM and closing at 11:00 PM each day. You will need a cook, someone to bus tables, wash dishes and keep the place clean, people to wait tables and take orders, and someone to run the cash register and supervise the people. You expect things to be slow during the break between lunch and dinner, but you will need to clean the place during that break. Someone will have to order the food and other supplies, check the delivery of those orders, keep the books, make the bank deposits, keep change in the cash register, schedule the workers, decide on the menu, and generally manage the operation. If you run the business yourself, you can handle all of the money, ordering, scheduling and decision making, but you will need people for everything else. You might be able to use part time people for all of the jobs. Let's say that you have worked in a restaurant in the area and you know that cooks get $10.00 per hour, wait staff get $4.00 per hour because they make tips, and everyone else makes $6.00 per hour. If you open at 11:00 AM, your cook and clean up staff will have to start at 10:00 to get the place ready. You will need two wait people during lunch, one during the slow time until dinner, and two during dinner, except for weekends, when you think you will need three during dinner. You need one person to handle busing and clean up at all times.

To get the cost estimate and to make sense of the staff needs, make a layout of the work schedule. That's just an hourly break down of each working day with the number of people and the kinds of jobs they must do penciled in for each hour. Add up all the hours and multiply them by the wage rates and you've got a good start on estimating the cost for wages. You will have to pay Social Security taxes and Unemployment taxes on the wages even if you don't provide any fringe benefits like insurance or pensions. That means that your actual labor cost will be at least 10% higher than the wages just to cover the taxes.

Don't forget to include a wage cost for yourself. How much would you expect to make if you took a job managing a business like the one you plan to start? You should put down at least that much money for yourself as part of your labor cost estimate. If the business can't support you, you don't want to start it.

## INVENTORY

Inventory is made up of the products which you will be selling. You will need suppliers to provide you with the start up inventory and to resupply you as you sell. If you've worked in a similar business for a while, you will know where to find suppliers, but it's not difficult. Suppliers list themselves in the yellow pages of the telephone book. You can find out about suppliers by talking to people in businesses like the one you're going to start. You can get price lists and delivery information by just calling suppliers and asking them for the information.

The difficult part of the process is deciding what inventory to buy and how much of it. If you don't have what people want, you can't sell it. If you buy things people don't want, then you tie up your money in things that won't sell and that makes it harder for you to buy the things that will sell. So, you can buy too much inventory, too little inventory, or the wrong kinds of inventory.

The problem can be very serious or less serious. Think about that restaurant again. If you don't buy enough food or drinks to make it through dinner one night, you might be able to run out to the grocery store and pick up some more. The things you buy that way will cost more than if you get them from your restaurant supplier, but at least you can get them quickly so that your customers won't get upset. You don't want them to get upset and decide not to come back.

On the other hand, if you're selling screen printed tee shirts, if you run out of size medium, black shirts, you'll probably have to call your supplier and order more. That could take a week or more to get them. Every customer who comes in during that time who wants a medium, black tee shirt will be disappointed. If it were size extra-extra large tee shirts, there might be very few people who come in asking for them. But those medium size shirts are likely to fit a large number of potential customers. That's why stores that sell clothes or shoes tend to have more of the middle sizes and fewer of the large and small sizes in stock. A lot of stores specialize in large or in small sizes just so they can reduce the amount of inventory they carry and make the process simpler.

How do you decide how much inventory to buy? Actually, it's a judgment call. That's why actual work experience in a similar business can be so valuable to you. Let's break the problem into two pieces. Buying replacement inventory after you have gotten started is much simpler. You decide how much to buy and the exact things to buy by watching what you sell and by talking to your customers. You want to stock the things they want. A good manager knows that watching what the customers buy and talking to them about what they're looking for is the best way to learn how to please them. If you monitor carefully, you will get better and better at choosing the right kinds and amounts of inventory.

When you first start up, you don't have the benefit of watching and talking to your customers. That means that you have to rely on your own judgment. The most important thing to remember is the image which you wanted your business to have. You must buy inventory which supports that image. Have you ever been in a store that looked as if it didn't have very much inventory? The store looked mostly empty? That creates a bad image. It makes people think the store has limited merchandise. They may not even bother to look to see whether the store is carrying what they want. How about stores with too much inventory? Haven't you seen stores where you couldn't find what you wanted because it was lost in a huge pile of inventory, or the racks were so full you couldn't pull an item out without making things fall?

It really goes back to your layout. You want the right amount of inventory to fill the space you have available, without over filling it. That means that being careful with how you organize the floor space will also help you to determine what you must buy initially. As you go through the process of laying out the store, lay out the inventory items which will be displayed on each rack, in each display case, and on each shelf. Keep a list. Visit competing stores and look at what they have. Do their stores look too full , or too cluttered or too empty? What do you want your business to look like? Make those diagrams and build up a list as you go. When you're done with the layout, you have a good idea of what your initial inventory will be. Now, you can call suppliers and find out what it will cost to stock the store. If you have to make adjustments because you don't have enough money, go back to your layouts. Change them around. Think about shrinking the store space by putting up a wall. You can always take it back down when the business grows.

## TALLYING ALL THE COSTS

We have talked about all of the various types of costs which you will have in starting your business. You now have some good ideas about what kinds of costs you will have and how much they will be. However, what you really have are estimates. Estimates are *always* wrong. That means that you need to plan for the problems with the estimates. How wrong can they be? Think about that as you go through each step of the process. Can the utilities be twice as much as the real estate agent estimates or half again as much? Will people really work for $4.00? Will you have to pay $5.00? Could you really need four people on Saturdays rather than the three people you have planned? Could your initial inventory cost 20% more than you think?

Every time you make a cost estimate, write it down and then consider how much higher it might be if your expectations are off a bit. Write down the higher figure as well as the first estimate you made. When you finish the process, you will have two cost estimates: a lower and a higher forecast. The real costs you will have are likely to fall between the two figures, but the range of costs will help you to plan better. You have to be ready to handle the higher cost figure, even while you work to achieve the lower cost figure.

## REVIEW

Revenues are the income which your business produces. Expenses or costs are the outlays of the business. The difference between the two is profit if the revenues are larger; loss is the expenses are larger. If revenues equal expenses, we say you are breaking even.

The important thing about expenses is how they behave over time. Fixed costs change very little from month to month. Variable costs go up or down as sales go up or down.

Predicting costs requires you to understand how a business operates. All businesses must have a location. There will be costs associated with that location: rent, heat, lights, water, telephone, insurance, etc. The business may or may not need employees. If it does, there are costs associated with the employees: salaries or hourly wages. The business may need equipment or machinery or furniture or fixtures. There are costs associated with all of these. Predicting costs means that you have to be able to predict what kinds of things a business will need to operate and what those things will cost.

The key to deciding how large a space a business needs and an important part of estimating costs is the lay out of the operation. This involves making a scale drawing of the interior of a business to locate everything required to operate the business.

Equipment is provided by businesses, called suppliers, who specialize in such products and can usually be purchased or leased, new or used. Leasehold improvements refer to the repairs or changes which you need to make to a building which you are renting. Leasehold improvements will belong to the landlord, the owner of the building, but you may need them to make the building usable.

Salaries and wages can be estimated by making a work schedule, which is an hourly break down of the working day which shows the number of people and the kinds of jobs they must do. This can be used to estimate the wages which will be required for the skill levels needed as well as the number of employees you will require. Don't forget to include wages for yourself.

Inventory is very hard to predict. Experience in an industry helps you to make such predictions. The amount and kinds of inventory is directly related to the image of the business and is a judgment call on the part of the owner.

Putting the costs together involves adding up all the predictions, but it goes beyond that. You need to consider the effects on the business of errors in your predictions. What if the rent is higher than you thought? What if you need more inventory than you thought? The overall cost prediction should be prepared as a range of estimates using higher and lower forecasts for the various costs your business will have.

## QUESTIONS, EXERCISES AND CASES

### Questions

1. Define the following terms:

   a. fixed costs
   b. variable costs
   c. layout
   d. leasehold improvements
   e. inventory
   f. revenue
   g. expenses
   h. breakeven
   i. salaries
   j. wages

2. Create a layout for a bicycle shop.

3. What are the two types of cost involved in a venture? Explain the differences.

4. How do leasehold improvements work and why?

### Exercise

Make a list of the costs associated with your venture. Be sure to include all of the aspects.

### Case

Trax & Trux, a new skateboard and bicycle outlet, opened its doors two weeks before Christmas. Barb and Don were excited about their new venture. As in all small towns, a large number of people had dropped in just to check out the shop. The kids were all excited and started revamping their Christmas lists on hearing of the new enterprise. Skateboards were back in and freestyle bikes were the most popular items on the lists that year.

Many parents, eager to finish their shopping, and thrilled that there was a place in town which sold such items, rushed to make purchases only to find that the store had been opened on very modest inventory. There were five freestyle bikes in pink with sold signs pinned to them and no complete skateboards. You purchased the assembly as well as the deck, wheels, trucks, clouds and decals. Most parents were at a loss. They had written down specific detail about the boards, knowing full well that only someone who knew boards could help them. Yet they remained unconvinced that assembly would result in the desired product.

Several inquiring minds asked the owners why they had decide to open a board and bike shop and they replied that there was a market in this area for replacement parts for these items and they had spent a great deal of time and energy on their son's behalf in trying to supply his needs.

The demand was indeed in the area but the frustration was also present. Parents needing Christmas toys had to resort to a larger town sixty-five miles away because Trax and Trux was an almost empty building. Replacement parts were possible but not that complete, perfect dream for Christmas morning.

Several months later, there was an exceptional amount of inventory. So much in fact that it was difficult to walk into the store without knocking against ice skates, jams, vans, and almost any part you could imagine. But Christmas was over!

1. What do you think customers felt at the lack of inventory at the opening?

2. Why do you think that the owners opened their doors when they did?

3. How well do you think the store is doing today and why?

4. Why do you suppose the situation ends with the statement "But Christmas was over!"?

5. What aspect of planning may have been short circuited in this case?

# CHAPTER TEN

## BREAKEVEN ANALYSIS

### INTRODUCTION

No business should ever be started without a break even analysis. It is really impossible to determine the viability of a new venture without investigating the volume of business which will be required for the venture to survive. Once that is determined, we must think about the probability that the venture can produce that volume. There are three steps involved in break-even analysis. First, we have to estimate the fixed costs which we are going to have. Then, we must estimate the variable costs as a percentage of sales. Finally, we must calculate the break-even point, the sales level which is required to cover all costs.

In the last chapter we talked about costs and how you estimate what they will be. A lot of the costs we talked about were start up costs. Things like the cost of leasehold improvements, buying the first supply of inventory, and things like that. To do break even analysis, we need to examine the costs that we have on a day to day basis. The idea is to figure out what the costs are going to be each year after the business has been started. The start up costs show us how much money we have to have to launch the new business. This will be the amount of money we need to save or borrow before we can get started. It is our financing needs and we will talk about how you make loan applications and find the start up financing in a later chapter. Right now, we want to talk about the fixed costs that you will have on a day to day basis in your business.

In the last chapter we said that fixed costs were those that did not change immediately as sales change. These are things like the rent, utilities, salaries, insurance premiums, and so on. For many businesses, virtually all the costs are fixed except those costs for replacement inventory. If you pay sales commissions, those will be variable, but most of your costs will not be. For some businesses selling services rather than products, there will be no variable costs at all and everything will be fixed.

## ESTIMATING FIXED COSTS

We need to estimate what the fixed costs are going to be for the entire year. We talked about how you make those estimates in the last chapter. Let's say that we want to start a hardware store. What are the steps in forecasting the fixed costs? In Table 1 we demonstrate that it is simply a result of lots of footwork. We need to keep lists and write the information, but mostly we just need to visualize what it will take for us to operate the store.

**Table 1**
**Estimating the Fixed Costs for a Hardware Store**

First, we visit a lot of hardware stores and we do a layout for our store, then we find a building to rent which fits our needs and is located in a good place. From the real estate agent, we find out that we will have to sign a three year lease which will set our rent payments at $2,000 per month. That will be $24,000 each year. We'll have to made two payments in advance.

The agent also said that we would probably have $180 per month for utilities, the heating, air conditioning, lights, water, trash pickup and so on. That's $2,160 each year.

We call the telephone company and find out that the telephone is going to cost $40 per month, plus long distance calls. We don't expect a lot of long distance calls. We will have to call our suppliers to make our orders, so we guess that we'll average $20 per month in long distance calls. That will make the annual cost about $720.

We call an insurance agent and we get an estimate for insurance of $2,200 per year.

We call an equipment supplier and find out that we can lease all of the display racks and bins, counters and everything else we need. They want three payments in advance, then the lease will be $300 per month, or $3,600 each year.

We call an office supplier and find out that they can sell us the computer, the software and the cash register which we need. They want a down payment of $500, then they will finance the rest for us and the loan payments are going to be $190 per month. That will make the annual cost $2,280.

We're going to need one additional person to work in the business with us during the whole time the store is open, 10 hours per day, 6 days per week. We will need a second person during the evening hours and on Saturday. That's five hours per day plus 10 hours on Saturday. That means a total of 95 hours per week or 4,940 hours per year. If we use part time people, we can get them for $5.50 per hour. That means that the payroll will be $27,170 per year. We talked to an accountant and we know that we will have to pay payroll taxes of about 10% on the salaries. That will make the salary cost $29,887 per year. We decide to round that off to $30,000.

We are going to have to be able to draw $20,000 per year out of the business for our living expenses. If we took a job somewhere else rather that starting this business, we would make more than that, but that's the minimum we can live on for the first year or so.

We called several hardware suppliers and we have estimated that we will need $30,000 of inventory when we open the store. That's a startup cost, but we will need to borrow a large part of it.

We called a sign company and we found out that putting up the kinds of signs we want on the building will cost $2,000.

We called a contractor and talked about leasehold improvements we want made to the building. They are going to run $11,000.

We checked with the state department of revenue and our business license will cost $50.

We have to make deposits on the water and the electricity. Those will be a total of $200. We have to have the phone installed and that will cost $300.

We asked an accountant about taking care of payroll and filing sales tax returns and state and federal income tax returns. She said it should run about $1,500 each year.

We're sure that we overlooked something, so we decide to add another $150 each month to our costs, just in case. This will be $1,800 per year.

Now, the startup costs are the advance rent payments, the down payments, the leasehold improvements, the sign, the deposits and the initial inventory. That's a total of $48,950. We will want to make sure we have some cash to carry us for a few weeks, so we add $5,000 to the start up costs to make $53,950. We have saved $10,000 and we can borrow the rest. The loan payments will be $980 per month, or $11,760 per year.

Looking at the fixed costs for the year from the table, we add up all the costs including the loan payments. That comes to $100,020, or rounding off, $100,000 per year. That's our estimate for the annual fixed costs for the hardware store.

## ESTIMATING VARIABLE COSTS

Now that we have the fixed costs, we need to think about variable costs. Those will change with small changes in sales volume. Since we are not going to pay any commissions, our only variable cost will be for replacement inventory. We talked to hardware store owners in various cities, we talked to the hardware suppliers, and we looked up hardware stores in the library and read about them. Our best information is that most hardware stores have a gross profit of 35%. Gross profit is the difference between sales and the cost of the inventory. For example, if we buy a power saw for $40 and sell it for $62.50, then we will make $22.50 over the cost of the saw. That would be a gross profit of 36% ($22.50/$62.50). We would say that the gross profit margin is 36% on the saw. This also means that the cost is 64% ($40/$62.50). If we buy #8 wood screws for $.01 each and we sell them for $.02 each, we will make a profit of $.01, or 50%. The cost would also be 50%. Each product that we sell will be the same. There will be different gross profit margins on different products. When people say that the average gross profit for the hardware store is 35%, they mean that the average of all the gross profit margins on all of the products we sell is 35%. This also means that the average cost for the inventory will be 65%.

You can think about the margins as the money you get to keep. If you sell $100 worth of products and you had to pay $60 for those products, you get to keep $40. That's a margin of 40%. The rest of the $100, the $60, is cost for the inventory; we can't keep it. We have to use that money to buy replacement inventory for the products which we sold. If we don't buy new products to replace those we sell, the store will soon run out of inventory. So, the sales we get must cover the replacement cost of the inventory, then we can keep the rest. If we expect an average gross profit margin of 35%, that means that we expect to keep 35% of our sales. That's $.35 out of $1.00 or $35 out of $100.

## CALCULATING THE BREAK EVEN POINT

The gross profit margin for our hardware store, 35%, is all we need to finish the break even analysis. Since we have no variable costs except inventory, the gross profit margin will tell us all we need to know. How much do the sales have to be to break even? Remember, we have to have $100,000 to cover the fixed costs, and we get to keep 35% of our sales. If we sell $100,000 worth of products, we will have $35,000 which we can use to cover the fixed costs (35% X $100,000). That's not enough. If we sell $200,000 worth of products, we will have $70,000 which we can use to cover fixed costs (35% X $200,000). That's still not enough. What we need is to find out the level of sales that will give us $100,000 to cover fixed costs. Notice that we have been multiplying the sales by the margin to show us how much we can keep. To find out how much the sales have to be to cover a particular level of fixed costs, we go the other way. That means that we divide the costs by the margin. It looks like this:

35% X Sales = $100,000
Sales = $100,000 / .35
Sales = $285,714

The sales we need to cover $100,000 of fixed costs are $285,714. That's the break even point. If we sell $285,714 worth of products and we make a gross profit margin of 35%, we will have gross profits of $100,000 (35% X $285,714). Since the fixed costs are expected to be $100,000, then the hardware store will have zero profits and zero losses. It will break even. The way we found that break even point was just to divide the costs by the margins.

There is a dangerous problem here for business owners. The break even point is an **estimate**. An estimate means that the number is *wrong*. What is even worse, we don't know how wrong it is. The only way that the hardware store will have exactly zero profits and zero losses at sales of $285,714 is if it has exactly $100,000 in fixed costs for the year and exactly 35% in gross profit for the year. It is far more likely that the store will have a little more or a little less than $100,000 in fixed costs. It is far more likely that the store will have a gross profit margin of a little more or a little less than 35%. Look what happens if we're off a bit in our estimates.

Let's say that the hardware store has to have a lot of sales to get people to come into a new place and to take business away from the competition. That could mean that we have to price everything a little less than the competition. If we do that, then our gross profit margin will be less than 35%. That was the average for hardware stores. If we have lower prices, we will have a lower gross profit. That's because our costs for the inventory items will be the same as everyone else. Remember that power saw we bought for $40? The saw sells for $62.50 in the hardware store down the street. During our sale to attract customers, we find that we have to sell it for $58.50. That would give us a gross profit of $18.50 or 32% ($18.50/$58.50). If we assume that we will have similar prices throughout the store, we will have an average gross profit margin of less than 35%. Look what happens if we get the forecast for fixed costs right, and the gross profit margin is actually 32%.

32% X Sales = $100,000
Sales = $100,000 / .32
Sales = $312,500

The last break even point was $285,714. The new forecast is $26,786 higher. Now, what if we missed the fixed cost estimate as well? What if we find that we can't get along with the number of employees we had planned? If we find that we have to have another person for the entire week, 60 hours, and we pay that person $5.50 per hour, we are going to need another $17,160 in salary plus the 10% payroll taxes. That means that the fixed costs will be closer to $119,000 than to $100,000. Use that number to calculate the break even and use the lower gross profit margin.

32% X Sales = $119,000
Sales = $119,000 / .32
Sales = $371,875

The first break even point was $285,714 and the second was $312,500. This new number is $86,161 higher than the first and $59,375 higher than the second. What is the real break even point? Sadly, we won't know what the real number is until the year is over. Then we can look at the actual results. What we want to do now, is to make two forecasts. The first forecast is based on our best guess of what the fixed costs and profit margins will be, $285,714. The second forecast should use higher estimates for fixed costs. What do you think the outside estimate for the costs will be? How high can they go? Think about each number in the estimate and consider how much higher it might be. Then, use a lower profit margin. How much lower is it likely to be? Use these pessimistic forecasts to make another estimate, $371,875. The real break even point is likely to fall somewhere between the two extremes. Now we have a good planning tool. We have a range of estimates for the break even point. Now let's talk about profits. We don't go into business to break even. We want to make a profit.

## MAKING A PROFIT

If we sell more than the break even point, we make a profit. After you pass the break even point, the gross profit becomes *real profit*. If we expect a gross profit margin of 35% and we think that it will take $300,000 in sales to break even, then everything over $300,000 produces a profit. Suppose we sell $400,000 of our inventory. That's $100,000 more than the break even point. The gross profit on that overage is $35,000 (35% X $100,000). That is the money we really get to keep. We've already covered the fixed costs with the first $300,000 in sales. Anything more becomes profit and it becomes ours.

We can actually build in a target level of profit and find out what the sales have to be to produce that. Think about the hardware store again. Let's say that we expect $119,000 in fixed costs for the year and we expect to have a gross profit margin of 32%. We have $20,000 built in to the fixed costs for our personal living expenses, but that's the minimum amount on which we can live. We really want to make much more than that. In fact, we might say that it's not worth the problems of starting the business unless we can make $100,000 per year. Since we have $20,000 built in to the fixed costs, that would mean that we want to have a profit of $80,000. How much would the sales have to be to produce that much?

$$32\% \text{ X Sales} = \$119{,}000 + \$80{,}000$$
$$\text{Sales} = \$199{,}000 / .32$$
$$\text{Sales} = \$621{,}875$$

In order to have a profit of $80,000, we would need sales of $621,875 assuming that our estimate of fixed costs and gross profit margin are good guesses. Now, we really have some good data for planning. We're really not willing to start this business unless it can produce more than $622,000 in sales each year. That's our target sales; the level of sales we really want to achieve.

## ADDITIONAL VARIABLE COSTS

In the hardware store example, we said that the only variable costs we would have would be to buy replacement inventory. What if that weren't true? What if we decided to pay the employees a sales commission? In addition to their salaries, we decide to pay a commission of 3% on every dollar of sales they make. Maybe we think this might be a good incentive to make them sell more.

If we look at the sales commission, we see that it means that we lose another 3% of each dollar of sales. With a gross profit margin of 32%, we were losing 68%. Now, we're losing 3% more. That means that we will get to keep 29% (32% - 3%). The break even point will change. If we use the $119,000 in fixed costs, the break even will be:

29% X Sales = $119,000
Sales = $119,000 / .29
Sales = $410,345

When we used the 32% margin, the break even was $371,875. The sales commission will raise the break even by $38,470. The commission will also raise the sales required to give us that $80,000 profit:

29% X Sales = $119,000 + $80,000
Sales = $199,000 / .29
Sales = $686,207

The old target sales were $621,875, but the commission raises it by $64,332.

Many businesses have variable costs like that sales commission. For example, many retail shops, especially those located in shopping malls have their rent based on sales. It is common for malls and shopping centers to charge you a flat amount each month for your rent and then to add on an extra charge of 2% or 3% of your sales. If you buy a franchise, then the franchisor will probably charge you a franchise fee which is a percentage of your sales. We'll talk about franchises in another unit. Right now, you just need to know that it's an arrangement that lets you use another company's name. In a franchise, you might have to set aside a flat percentage of sales to cover advertising costs as well. Many of the fast food franchises charge a franchise fee of 3% or 4% of sales and then require you to put another 3% of sales into advertising.

If you have variable expenses other than inventory costs, then the break even and target sales are calculated the same way. We just want the percentage of sales which you get to keep. We divide that into the estimate for your fixed costs or fixed costs plus profit to find the break even point or the target sales.

There are actually other expenses which have a variable nature, but which are treated as part of the fixed costs. For example, the electricity bill is made up of two parts. You are charged a flat rate each month plus a charge for each kilowatt of electricity you actually use. That means that part of the electricity bill seems to be a variable cost. We ignore things like that because the electricity bill really won't change with small changes in your sales volume. You have to have the lights on the entire time that the store is open regardless of what you sell. What we really want is to identify those costs that will change with small changes in sales and call those variable. Then we want to know what those variable costs are as a percentage of sales. The rest of the sales we get to keep. If there are no variable costs besides those associated with inventory, then we call the part we get to keep the gross profit margin. If there are additional variable costs, then we call the part we get to keep, the contribution margin.

## SERVICE VENTURES

Just because a business sells services rather than inventory doesn't mean that it has no variable costs. There may still be commissions such as in a real estate agency. The labor costs themselves might be variable as in a construction company. If any costs vary with small changes in sales volume, then we want to identify those as variable costs and turn them into percentages of sales so that we can find the contribution margin.

The danger here is to assume that some kinds of costs *will* vary. For example, let's consider the case of a garage. If you run a garage and you pay the mechanics on an hourly basis, then their salaries appear to be variable. If you send people home when there is no work to do, or stop their wages when they are not working directly on a repair job, then the wages truly are a variable expense. However, it must be a real situation. Most garages actually pay mechanics flat salaries even though they may be stated as hourly wages. What actually happens is that the mechanics work harder or slower as necessary to fill up the day and take care of the work that must be done. Since skilled mechanics are hard to find and hard to keep, you can't afford to send them home when business falls off for a short while. That means that their wages are really a fixed cost.

In some businesses, especially those that employ low skilled people, the employees will be sent home or docked if they are not actually working. Fast food restaurants frequently handle their people that way. In other businesses, like construction companies, people are hired for a particular job. When the project is finished, the job is over and wages stop. For those businesses, the wages are variable costs.

The important point is to separate the costs so that the fixed costs will be properly estimated. In fact, if you have any doubts, it's usually better to treat a cost as though it were fixed. The most conservative approach to break even analysis is to have more fixed costs rather than less. That way, you are less likely to underestimate the break even or target sales. For that reason, if a cost is hard to identify as variable or it's hard to determine what percentage of sales the variable cost will be, just add it to the fixed costs. The only error that can result is an overestimate of the break even and target sales. Since it is an estimate that we are making, we're not interested in trying to find a right answer. That can't happen. What we want is to make a forecast that is useful. A forecast that is higher that what we actually will require is more useful than one which is lower because it will give us a higher objective for which to plan.

## ADDITIONAL USES

Break even analysis has many uses other than finding break even points or target sales for a new venture. We can use it to help decide whether to open a new location, add a new line of merchandise, drop a line of merchandise, or almost any kind of business decision. The key relationship is simply that cost divided by margin yields sales. Let's say that the sales representative from the telephone company comes into our hardware store. She wants to sell us advertising in the Yellow Pages of the telephone book. For a half page ad on the same page as our listing, it's going to cost $6,000 per year, but they will add it to the telephone bill so that it will be easy to pay. Should we buy the advertising? If we know that our contribution margin is going to be 29%, then we can make an informed decision. Think about how much business the ad will have to bring to us in order to pay for itself. It looks like this:

29% X Added Sales = $6,000
Added Sales = $6,000 / .29
Added Sales = $20,690

The calculation says that we will have to gain an extra $20,690 in sales from the yellow pages ad in order to pay for the ad. If we expect to make a profit on the ad, we will have to sell more than that. If the average customer spends $20, that would mean that the ad would have to bring us 1,034 customers whom we would not get without the advertisement ($20,690 / $20). Do you think that is likely to happen? If you have doubts, then buying the advertising will not be a wise decision.

## REVIEW

Break even analysis helps to determine the feasibility of starting your own business. No business should ever be started without performing a break even and yet they are started that way, every day. It is far better to decide not to go into business than to try and fail. Break even analysis can help you understand the probability of failure or success.

First, the prospective owner must identify the costs and estimate what they will be. Fixed costs will include such things as the building, leasehold improvements, the utilities, insurance, licenses, equipment, office supplies, employees, owner's draw, signs, professional fees of accountants and lawyers, etc.

Variable costs are those that change with the sales volume and may be difficult to identify. If variable costs are too hard to estimate, we can look up the average gross profit margin for businesses like ours in the library. This margin is a good substitute for the contribution margin ratio because it includes the cost of inventory and most start up businesses have few variable costs beyond inventory.

It is possible for variable costs to occur in service companies and businesses without inventory. The key to identifying them is to understand how costs will change with sales volume.

The break even point is an estimate, not an absolute value. It is a planning tool, no more, no less. The best approach is to calculate several break even points by adjusting your expectations for fixed costs, gross profit margin or contribution margin. The result will be a range of estimates and the real break even point is likely to fall within that range.

Making a profit is our purpose in going into business so what does it take to be successful? We can modify break even analysis to include a desired profit level and forecast the target sales required to be successful using the same techniques.

Break even analysis techniques can also be used for other than finding the break even point or target sales for a new venture. The analysis can be used to decide such things as whether to open a new branch location, add a new line of merchandise, drop a line of products, to evaluate the success of advertising and promotions, and a host of other day to day uses.

# QUESTIONS, EXERCISES AND ASSIGNMENTS

## Questions

1. What are the steps in break-even analysis?

2. Distinguish between fixed and variable costs.

3. Why do you want to do more than breakeven?

4. Why should you not put tremendous faith in breakeven values?

5. How are target sales predicted and why are they so important?

6. Indicate all the uses of breakeven points.

## Exercise

Assume that you are considering the startup of a small bookstore. There are virtually no variable costs expected beyond those associated with the inventory. Your planning has resulted in the following estimates:

| | |
|---|---:|
| Fixed Costs for the First Year: | \$84,000 |
| Industry Average Gross Profit Margin: | 28% |

1. What would be the break-even point?

2. What would be the target sales necessary to produce a profit of \$56,000?

## Case

Marilyn is considering opening a small boutique with unusual gift items. Everyone loves her original ideas for parties and meetings. But she is very concerned about the risk. Marilyn has a friend who started a bridal shop several years ago and she almost lost her home as a result of its failure. Everyone had thought a bridal shop was a good idea as well, but most of her friends didn't need her services and neither did enough people in her small town. She had used her house as collateral and when the sales didn't come, the bank wanted its collateral. She had finally worked out a payment plan for the business, but it was taking her ten years to pay for her mistake.

Marilyn did not want the same costly mistake to happen to her. She had heard from a consultant who presented a seminar on starting businesses that you should always perform a breakeven analysis before investing your money, so she decided to perform one.

First she considered all of the fixed expenses for the first year:

| | | |
|---|---|---|
| Lease (store) | $ 8 ,400.00 | |
| All utilities | 2,400.00 | |
| Insurance | 1,200.00 | |
| Salaries (self) | 20,000.00 | |
| Fringe benefits | | 3,000.00 |
| Miscellaneous | | 1,200.00 |
| 15% of salaries | | |
| Total Fixed Costs | | $ 36,200.00 |

Then, she estimated the average gross profit ratio from library sources:

| | |
|---|---|
| Contribution Margin Ratio | 36% |

Calculate the breakeven for Marilyn and advise her as to whether she should open her boutique.

Are there fixed costs which Marilyn may have overlooked? If so, what are they? (Hint: How many hours do you think the shop should be open? Can Marilyn handle that alone?) Recalculate the breakeven using your own fixed cost estimate. What is your recommendation after the recalculation? If you don't think the venture is feasible as it stands, what do you think that Marilyn could do to make her dream come true?

# CHAPTER ELEVEN

## DETERMINING FEASIBILITY

### INTRODUCTION

Can the business you want to start support itself and provide you with the kind of living that you want? That's what we mean by feasible. We have talked about finding the break even and target sales for your new business, and that is a major step in answering this question. A feasible business is one which generates enough revenue to cover all its costs and can still provide the owner with the income he or she desires. It can produce the target sales which the owner needs. That means that making a decision about the feasibility of your business is the most important decision you can make during the start up phase. It's not just a case of deciding whether to start the business or not. Obviously, you don't want to begin the venture if it can't provide what you want. However, it may be that you can make the business feasible by making some changes in how the business operates, where it is located, what it sells, or some other aspect. If you start the business without knowing that it has some problem in how it's set up, you could find yourself out of business before you have a chance to discover what's wrong and correct it. That's why feasibility assessment is so important.

## DETERMINING MARKET SHARE

After we have gotten a range of estimates for the break even point and for the target sales for our business, we must decide whether the market area in which we intend to locate will support the volume. Sometimes that's easy and sometimes it's hard. Think about that hardware store example again. The last estimate we made was for a target sales level of $686,207. If your county is large enough, the local Chamber of Commerce, or its equivalent, will have statistics about the sales of various types of products. Hardware products may be on the list. If you have data like that available, the job is easy. Let's say that you go to the Chamber and find out that there were total sales of $3,800,000 in hardware in your county last year. That means that you need about 18% of the total market for your store to be feasible ($686,207 / $3,800,000). If there are four hardware stores in town now, yours will make five stores. If you did everything as well as the other stores did, you ought to be able to get 20% or 1/5th of the market. You don't need that much, you only need 18%, so your store appears to be feasible. If there are nine stores in town now, and yours will make ten, then you can only count on getting about 10% or 1/10th of the market. You need more than that, you need 18%. That means that you will have to draw almost twice as much business as an average store. If the store you are planning to start is the same size as the other stores in the area, then you are going to have problems. If you plan to start with twice as much inventory in a store twice as large as the others, then your operation could still be feasible. The key is to find out how much of the market you need in your operation. That is your market share. Just divide your sales forecast by the total sales in the market. Then you just need to consider how your business will affect the competition. If you need a 50% market share, then you had better be in position to take that much. You will have to have 50% of the total inventory in town and you must be located so that you can get 50% of the customers to come to your shop instead of your competitors.

## DETERMINING MARKET SIZE

Frequently, there are no statistics available for you to use in finding a market share. Your business may be the first of its kind in the market area or your county may not keep records which would allow you to find the sales for your kind of business. What do you do in a case like that? We fall back upon looking at the size of the market.

Even if the local chamber of commerce doesn't keep the right kind of records, we can always find out the population of our market area. The reports prepared by the Bureau of the Census break down population by SMSA or Standard Metropolitan Statistical Area. This information is available in the public library or on the Internet at www.census.gov, and there are international equivalents which can provide this same data for most nations in the world. The data that the Bureau of the Census collects will tell you the population in your SMSA, and it will break down the information to show you population by income level and various other kinds of information.

Recently, a couple asked us for help in determining whether their idea for a new business was feasible. They wanted to buy a franchise for a fish specialty fast food restaurant and start up in a small, rural county. There was no data in that county that would allow us to find market share information. The franchise required 5% of sales for franchise fees plus 4% of sales for advertising fees. This lowered the contribution margin a great deal. When we worked up the estimates for getting the business started, we found that it needed about $500,000 in sales each year to break even. We estimated that each customer would spend about $8 on average for a meal. Using that estimate, we converted the sales forecast to an estimate of daily traffic.

$500,000 / $8.00 = 62,500 customers per year
62,500 / 365 days = 171 customers per day

That estimate means that the restaurant would have to *average* 170 customers each day. Busy days averaged with slow days, week ends averaged with week days, the business needs 170 customers per day or, 1,190 per week in order to break even. Next, we looked at the population data.

The population of the county was just over 30,000 people. Not only that, the population of the county was predominantly poor. Less than half the families in the county had incomes over $25,000 per year. We thought that eating out would be a luxury for the poor families and therefore our real market was centered in the families with $25,000 or more in annual income. That was about 15,000 people. Of course, we cannot expect everyone to eat out at a restaurant each day. If we assume an average of three times per week, then that is 45,000 meals per week (3 X 15,000), or about 6,430 meals per day (45,000 / 7). Now our required break even point was 170 customers per day. With a market demand of 6,430 meals per day, we would have to attract about 2.6% of the market each day:

170 customers per day / 6,430 estimated meals = 2.6%

Does that sound like a lot? It depends on the competition. We checked and found that there were 34 restaurants in the county. Several of them were not doing very well, but some seemed to have lots of business. If our restaurant could draw an equal share of the potential market along with the competition, then what could we expect to draw?

6,430 estimated meals / 35 restaurants = 184 customers per day

That sounds like it might be feasible, but our restaurant is a fast food fish house; a specialty restaurant. That means that it appeals to a smaller segment of the market. From another perspective, people are not likely to eat in a specialty restaurant as often as they do in other types of restaurants. If the average person eats at fish restaurants half as often as at restaurants that serve meat and chicken, then we cannot expect to draw a full market share. If our potential draw is half that of regular restaurants, then we can only expect about 92 customers per day, and that is not enough to reach our break even.

An important part of this story is that we did *not* tell the couple not to start the business. We recommended that they find a new location in a more populous county and start the business there. That is the real strength of feasibility analysis. It not only helps you decide whether you can be successful, it helps you in planning all aspects of the business, including its location.

## CHANGES TO ENHANCE FEASIBILITY

As you can see from the last example, you can usually make changes to the business plan to make it become more feasible. You can find a new location with different population statistics, or you can change the size of the operation or the number of people it will employ, in order to lower the costs of operation. The key is, you must be flexible. If you really want to start your own business, you must be willing to go where the market is, and to appeal to what the market wants.

Not everyone is willing to do that. Not long ago we spoke with a young woman who had started a bakery in a small town. She loved baking and had dreamed of having her own business, so, after high school, she decided to combine the two. Her parents loaned her enough money to get started and she found a building to rent, and launched her business. She was having trouble making ends meet. She was working very hard and doing everything herself to save money. She got up at 4:00 every morning and baked for four hours before opening the shop at 8:00. She was a wonderful baker and her pastries were really great, but she had been in business for a year and still couldn't support herself. She was having to live at home with her parents to make ends meet. We looked at her operation and calculated its break even point. She had not done such an analysis before she opened her shop. After our analysis, we just did not find enough population in that small town to support her and the four other bakeries with which she competed. We suggested that she move her shop about 60 miles away to the nearest large city. With her skill and the larger market, we thought that she could do very well.

When we gave her our advice, she was incensed. She let us know that this was her home town. She did not want to leave. She wanted to know how to make the bakery successful right here. We tried to explain that no matter how good her products were, people just don't buy fresh baked goods every day. That means that you have to have a large enough market to let you be successful and such a market just did not exist in her home town. The other bakeries in town did not depend solely upon baked goods. Three of the bakeries were part of grocery stores and the fourth bakery also handled sandwiches, salads, and other lunch items. There was no way to reduce her costs any more than she had done, so the only alternative was to move to a market area which could support her.

As you might guess, the young woman did not take our advice. She found another location in town which had a slightly lower rent, and continued to try to make it in her home town. Less than a year later, she had nearly worked herself to death and finally closed the business.

## COMPLETELY UNIQUE VENTURES

One of the dreams that many people have is starting a new business which has never existed before. You have probably read many stories about such people. The story of Apple Computers and Steve Jobs and Steve Wozniak is such a story. They started an entirely new industry, the personal computer industry. Maybe it's Fred Smith and Federal Express, or the story of Ted Turner and his cable television business. Again, these were entirely new businesses which had never existed before. How do you decide if a business like that is feasible before you start it?

Break even analysis can help because it will let you understand what you're going to have to do in terms of volume, but it is not really very useful in helping you to decide whether the business can be successful. For ventures like that, you have to be willing to take the risk. A great deal of the real success that these pioneers had was based on the fact that they started their businesses at the right time. People were ready to buy what they had to sell.

If Jobs and Wozniak had tried to start Apple five years earlier than they did, they would not have survived long enough to be successful. The market just wasn't ready. Most of the pioneers understood that. They had to judge the timing of their ventures and the potential for a market. Then, they had to have faith in their ability and be willing to take the risk. It doesn't always work, but we don't hear about the failures. Henry Ford tried to start a company to build racing cars before he started Ford Motor Company. There was no market for racing cars, and he went bankrupt. A few years later, he decided that the United States was ready for a company which built family cars for the average family. This time, he was right. Many of the pioneers failed several times before they were successful.

## THE SUBJECTIVE DECISION

Break even analysis can never make a decision for you. All it can do is help you understand the situation better. In the final analysis, it's always a judgment call, a subjective decision. Do you think that you can attract the volume of business in this market that it takes to be successful? Even so, the analysis helps you to understand what that volume of business will be. If our baker friend had understood more about business and had conducted a break even analysis before she started her business, she would not have been surprised when she began to experience trouble in making ends meet.

The problem is that too many people just don't think about the practical matters involved. If they did, then a great deal of heart ache and financial loss could be avoided. The good news is that if you're willing to do the work and the planning, and you're willing to go where the market is, you can be successful.

## REVIEW

A feasible business is one which generates enough revenue to cover all its costs and can still provide the owner with the income he or she desires. That means that feasibility is the true determinant of success at the startup of a business venture.

After determining the break even points and target sales, the market area has to be seriously considered. Will this business survive in this area at this location? The analysis tells us how large the sales have to be, and then we need to see if the market can produce that many sales. Population statistics and demographics can help in this determination.

Converting the target sales into market share data can be very useful. Can the pie be sliced any smaller and still have room for success? Can you take enough market share away from the established competition to make your venture successful?

Even if statistics are not readily available about market share, the population data from the Standard Metropolitan Statistical Area can be used to approximate the potential for success. Common sense is the key to the determination about whether this market area and location can support your business venture.

What is not feasible in one market area may be perfect for another. If you really want to start your own business, you must be willing to go where the market is, and to appeal to what the market wants.

If you choose a new business which has never been done in your area before, the potential for success may be tremendous, but so is the potential for failure. To prove yourself in a market never defined and to create a demand for a product or service with which the market is unfamiliar is a risky proposition. Break even analysis and feasibility studies may give you valuable information, but timing is much more important than all the data we can generate. The public has to be ready for what we propose.

Unfortunately, there is no crystal ball nor right answer as to what is feasible or what is not. The best answer is to use all the tools at your disposal, examine all the factors, try to eliminate some of the risk, then make a judgment call. The decision to start a business is yours. The chance for success is greater when you have used the tools properly so that your decision is based upon reality, not merely dreams.

# QUESTIONS, EXERCISES AND ASSIGNMENTS

**Questions**

1. What is meant by the term feasible with regard to an entrepreneurial venture?

2. Why is feasibility the most important decision that one can make during the startup phase?

3. Is it possible to *make* a business feasible? Why or why not?

4. What does one do if there is no market share data in a given location? What does this mean?

5. Explain the following statement: Break even analysis can never make a decision for you.

**Exercise**

1. Look at your home town in the light of ideas for various types of entrepreneurial ventures. Identify several types of ventures which you think might be developed which could be feasible in your home town, and identify several other types of ventures which you do not think could be made to be feasible.

**Case**

Al Kitchen was excited. He was going to own his own business just as soon as he got all the paperwork squared away. He was young and enthusiastic and had his whole life ahead of him. Just a few short weeks ago, he had been discharged from the Army and when he couldn't find a job immediately that appealed to him and for which he was qualified, he decided why not start his own business and be his own boss.

He had always enjoyed cooking and his grandmother had passed down several recipes which were out of this world. That's what gave him the idea one day when he came home early from job hunting and had some delicious home cooking waiting for him to ease his troubled spirits. And it had! It had given Al this wonderful idea about what to do with his future. The job hunting was not going well and he had to do something soon because he needed to support his wife and little boy.

He started making his plans. There was a new mall going up outside of town and all the spaces had not yet been leased. He would go talk to them and see what he could do. After all if he only served soup, it couldn't be too expensive a proposition, could it? And, too, there wasn't any other place like this in town, so it was bound to be successful. He would start small and then grow.

Al decided to make this a family business. His sister and wife would help him out with the cooking and waiting on customers. He could also cut down on expenses by using paper and plastic products rather than dishes that had to be washed. If things went really well, he would expand to sandwiches and hire someone to take over for his wife from time to time.

Al had already contacted the mall officials to inquire about leasing possibilities and had learned that the only site he could afford was the one that leased for $10 per square foot and measured 500 square feet in the shape of an ell in an interior corner of the mall. He was to sign the lease quickly if he was to get the space because the mall manager was anxious to have all the floor space assigned within the next few weeks. Al was tempted to go ahead and sign the lease right there on the spot rather than risk losing out to someone else. He had $5,000 mustering out pay from the service that he had put in the bank when he got home, but his wife had made him promise not to sign anything until they had had time to discuss it more fully.

When Al got home full of visions of grandeur and dreams of making this small area just the beginning, he and his wife sat down and started discussing how much money would be needed in addition to the lease payment. There was kitchen equipment to lease, paper products and supplies to buy, operating expenses, and leasehold improvements and furniture. Since this was a new mall, there had been no other tenants in this space before and he needed to start from scratch.

After a very confident trip to the bank, he was declined the $20,000 loan he requested. It seemed that the loan officer didn't share his dream of success. The loan officer had asked him some searching questions about things he had never considered. The one that bothered him most was about breakeven analysis. The banker asked how much soup Al had to sell to breakeven. This had him worried. The banker had suggested that he call an assistance agency which gave that kind of advice free. Al called the Small Business Development Center and decided that before he gave up his savings, he would go see those people. He would see whether they thought he could be successful and find out exactly what his breakeven was. Surely, they would see how great his idea was and maybe they would even help him get a loan.

Al received help from the SBDC in developing estimates for the expenses which the business would incur in its operation. They also established forecasts for prices and average ticket levels for the customers. The forecasts are listed below.

Examine the information and prepare a breakeven analysis for the operation. Be sure to calculate breakeven in sales dollars and in number of customers. Also calculate the breakeven in sales and number of customers per day. This will help in determining reasonableness and attainability of the forecast.

| | | |
|---|---|---|
| Average Ticket per Customer | $ 3.50 | |
| Fixed Cost Estimates for the First Year: | | |
| Lease (store) | $ 5,000.00 | |
| Lease (kitchen equipment) | 2,400.00 | |
| All utilities | 2,600.00 | |
| Insurance | 1,500.00 | |
| Salaries (wife & sister) | | 12,000.00 |
| Owner's Draw | | 20,000.00 |
| Fringe benefits (15% of salaries) | | 4,800.00 |
| Total Fixed Costs | | $ 48,300.00 |
| Variable Cost Estimates for the First Year: | | |
| Food (industry average) | | 60% of sales |
| Paper & utensils | | $.10 per customer |
| Variable Cost Ratio | | $.10 / $3.50 = 3% |
| Total Variable Costs | | 63% of sales |
| Contribution Margin | | 37% |

On the basis of your analysis, do you think the venture is feasible? Be sure to consider how many meals Al needs to serve each day, but remember how many serving hours he will actually have each day. That is, how long does lunch last? While you think about that, consider how long it will actually take to serve a customer.

# CHAPTER TWELVE

## MARKETING TECHNIQUES

### INTRODUCTION

Marketing is frequently confused with advertising. Since Shakespeare's day the focus of the sales effort has been on praising the goods or services held for sale. Marketing is much more than advertising. An important part of any marketing effort is the planning and execution of effective advertising, but marketing must go beyond advertising in order to be effective. The goal of marketing is to sell goods or services. These things are actually sold through a coordinated effort which includes every aspect of your operation.

### ADVERTISING

Advertising is the most visible part of the marketing operation of a firm. The average person is bombarded with advertising every day. Television, radio, print media, direct mail, billboards; advertising is everywhere. Despite the broad range of media, there are really only two types of advertising which a firm can do: **product/service advertising** and **image advertising**. Both are aimed at selling. That's all that advertising is: a sales pitch.

Much of the advertising which you see is aimed at promoting a particular product or service. That's because it is easier to sell a specific item: you can talk about that item's features, its price, its desirability, etc. This can be broadened to advertising which is aimed at several items at once. For example, several items might be placed on sale and advertising used to promote that fact. It can be highly specific. It may take several commercials or advertising spots to convey the entire message on a single product.

The outdoor advertising efforts of *Burma Shave* are a classic example. Numerous signs located alongside the highway were used with each sign containing a few words of the overall message. These signs would appear sequentially some distance apart with the effect of drawing a traveler's attention to what were at first meaningless phrases in an attempt to find out what the message was. Regardless of how specific or general, regardless of the media used, advertising for a product or service is the easier approach because we are dealing with something tangible. There can be some spill over between the two types of advertising, but the primary objective of **product/service advertising** is to create a desire in the minds of the customers for a specific item.

There is also a risk associated with product/service advertising. If the advertising is successful and a demand for an item is created, there is no guarantee that the customers will use our business as the source of supply to satisfy their demand. Most large firms attempt to create a brand image which distinguishes their wares from competitors. Most small businesses are unable to use such a strategy because of the cost and time that creating such an image requires. Consequently, for a small business, creating a demand for an item can carry great risk because people may decide to buy the item from a competitor or to acquire a near substitute.

Frequently, price of an item is used as part of the advertising in an attempt to channel demand to a specific company. Consider a grocery store advertising its meat. If the advertising is effective, people seeing it will buy more meat but not necessarily from the store doing the advertising. You can attempt to isolate the demand through a variety of techniques including reduced prices or sales, coupons, trading stamps, etc. Another device for isolating the demand is through image advertising either in conjunction with the product/service advertising or in separate advertising efforts.

In **image advertising**, we are promoting the reputation and image of the firm rather than the products or services of that firm. There can be a mingling of the two types of advertising in that some aspects of the products may be a part of the image promotion. For example, the image advertising could stress product/service quality, price, availability, etc. Nevertheless, the primary objective of image advertising is the establishment of a specific set of beliefs about the company in the minds of its customers. The primary benefit is the isolation of demand. That means that we wish the demand for items created through product/service advertising to benefit our firm rather than our competitors.

In order for image advertising to be effective, the image of the firm must be consistently established throughout all phases of the operation. If the image we wish to portray is one of high quality, high service, then the firm must be structured so that this is always the case. If the image is one of low cost, no frills, then the firm must be consistent with that image in all of its phases. Some form of image advertising is valuable in any promotional activities not only because it helps localize demand but because it forces a firm to analyze its image and consciously consider cultivating that image over time.

## ADVERTISING MEDIA

**Media** refers to the vehicle used to deliver an advertising message to customers. Television, radio and newspaper advertising spring to mind immediately, but there are many other types of media. In fact the array of advertising media available is staggering. Table 1 lists some of the kinds of advertising outlets which exist.

Table 1 is by no means a complete list. In fact, the type of media which can be used is limited only by your imagination. Be careful to think any unusual steps through carefully. You wouldn't want one of the basketball players to fall off a mule and get hurt.

Table 1: Advertising Media

- Television (don't forget cable TV carriers)
- Radio
- Newspaper (don't forget school papers)
- Internet
    - Banner ads
    - Search Engine Optimization
    - Search Ads
- Outdoor
    - Billboards
    - Signage
        - Fixed signs
        - Lighted and moving signs
    - Transit
        - Buses
        - Cabs
        - Trains
        - Personal Automobiles
    - Houses
    - Barns and Barn Roofs
    - Fences
    - Flyers for Car Windshields
    - Hand Bills passed out to pedestrians and shoppers
    - Signs carried by individuals
    - Individuals wearing costumes
    - Airplanes towing signs
- Indoor
    - Grocery Stores
    - Store Windows
    - Signs and Placards and Posters

Table 1: Advertising Media (continued)

- Indoor (continued)
  - Card Racks
    - Welcome Centers and Rest Areas
    - Tourist Bureaus and Chambers of Commerce
    - Hotels, Restaurants
  - Point of Sale Displays
- Demonstrations
  - Product or Service Demos
    - In your shop
    - On street corners
    - In other businesses
- Magazines
- Trade Journals
- High School Annuals
- Programs for ball games
- Gifts, Premiums, Coupons (sold or given away)
  - Balloons
  - Pens
  - Umbrellas
  - Seat Cushions
  - T shirts and sweat shirts
  - Cups
  - Hats
  - Almost anything you can think of
- Special Events
  - Radio Shows
  - Celebrities
  - Ball Games and Competitions
    - Basketball played by people riding mules
    - Our guys against their guys
- Sponsoring
  - Charity events
  - Fund raising events
  - School and amateur ball teams, clubs, groups, etc.
- Yellow Pages and Directories

The problem from a marketing perspective is the selection of a medium which will provide maximum penetration of the target market for the dollars expended. It is not enough for a large number of people to be exposed to the advertising; what is required is the exposure of a large number of people in your target market. For example, television is generally considered to have the broadest penetration of any type of advertising media because such large numbers of people watch it. However, if your customers seldom watch TV, it may not be an appropriate medium for your advertising. To complicate the matter, advertising is frequently priced on the basis of the number of people who view the advertising, and that can make television very expensive. The reality is that it does not matter how many people view your advertising message; what matters is how many people in your target market view your advertising message.

The problem is complicated by the timing and location issue. In TV and radio advertising, the time of day and day of week is a factor in the effectiveness of the advertising. Commercials during the middle of the day on TV may be most effective if the target market is primarily homemakers, but commercials during sports games may be more appropriate for some products or services. On the other hand, advertising on news channels, sports channels, cartoon channels, etc., might be more appropriate. Radio commercials during the 6:00AM to 8:00AM period and 4:00PM to 6:00PM period are best for catching people on the way to and from work, but may not be as effective as late night broadcasts depending upon the target market. Of course, the variety of radio stations, rock to classical, complicate the issue even more. Most radio stations have viewer profiles which can aid in targeting your message, but that presupposes that you know who your target market is.

With print media, location and timing are still issues. The Sunday newspaper gets a larger readership than any other day of the week, while location of the advertising within the paper can affect the likelihood of a member of the target market seeing it. With magazines and journals, location of the advertising is also a factor. It is no accident that the back cover of a magazine is the most expensive advertising spot. In addition, the size of the advertising and its location on the page, as well as its wording and layout, can affect its likelihood of being read.

Almost every type of media is affected by timing or location issues. Even flyers placed on car windshields can be more effective at certain times, such as on pay days of major employers in the area. In addition, all media is affected by the design of the advertising itself. Surely you have noticed that some billboards draw your attention while you can drive by others without being aware that you have passed them.

The various combinations of all of the factors of timing, location, advertising design and type of media are almost limitless. How can you wade through all this to find the best way to spend your advertising dollars? Actually, what is required is more an understanding of your target market than of advertising. If you fully understand who your customers are, what their habits and preferences are, where and when they work and where and when they play, then you can begin to plan the best way to reach them. The more detailed your knowledge about your target market, the more effective your advertising can be. However, the less you know about your market, the less effective advertising will be. This is also true when applied to developing the proper image for your company. The more you know about a market to which you wish to appeal, the more effectively you can design a strategic posture or business image which will appeal to that market.

Be careful. The advertising and image selection and design must appeal to your target market, not to you. The biggest and most frequent mistake made by new business owners is the confusion of the preferences of the owner with the preferences of the customers. You must put yourself in the shoes of your customers; you must develop a keen understanding of them and of the people and businesses you will cultivate as customers.

How many times have you seen commercials in which the owner of a small business uses his or her children in the spot? What purpose can that serve? The answer is that it serves self satisfaction, not customer satisfaction. Advertising will not automatically attract customers. In fact, it can do the reverse. Poor advertising can discourage would be customers and drive away existing customers. In a recent election in our home town, there was a run off required between two candidates vying for a position on the county school board. One candidate, who happened to be the incumbent in office, received about 49% of the vote in the first election, while his nearest competitor in a field of five people received about 20% of the votes cast. During the campaigning for the run off, the leading candidate used a flyer with a photograph and covered virtually every car windshield in the county with those flyers. Unfortunately, the photograph was unflattering, to say the least. The quality of reproduction was poor and the candidate appeared haggard and unshaven in the flyer. To top that off, the flyer carried virtually no message: no statement of position on any issue was made. The flyer simply exhorted the reader to vote for the candidate because he had experience on the job. On election day, the incumbent was soundly defeated. We'll never know whether he would have won if that flyer had not been circulated, but we can say that it certainly did not aid his campaign. The same thing can and does happen to businesses. Poorly designed, poorly planned advertising can be worse than no advertising at all.

You must also be careful about what your advertising promises. Recently, a local grocery store displayed a special price on T bone steaks on its marquee. Several customers were heard to complain upon entering the store, that the special price was for steaks which had turned dark. Fresher steaks were displayed side by side with the sales meat and these looked better but were priced higher. The store probably lost many customers permanently as a result of that mistake.

Sometimes difficulties with promises can be more subtle. A local automobile dealer is well known in the community for his television commercials in which he always displays several used cars with special prices. The owner does the commercials personally and always ends the spot by saying, "Come and see me and let's make a deal." After observing several years of highly successful operations using those commercials, another dealer in town decided to use the same approach. He began to air TV spots in which he displayed used cars with special prices and ended the commercial with an exhortation to "Come and see me for a real deal." After a few months of those spots, the dealer was reduced to the level that he could no longer afford TV commercials at all. It seems that a customer walking on his lot could never see the owner at all. Every customer was met by sales people and the owner took no part in the sales effort. In the case of the successful car dealer, virtually every customer would at least see and speak to the owner and a large number of them would be handled personally by the owner. The hidden promise in both of the commercials was an opportunity to bargain directly with the owner rather than a sales representative without the power to 'deal'. Only one of the dealers was living up to that promise.

The image which your business has and wishes to portray must also be clear in the advertising. If the advertising works and customers are attracted to the business, they must not be surprised. If they are led to develop one image of the business through the commercial and discover another image when buying from the firm, they will become confused and may well cease to be a customer. The image is affected by the choice of media as much as it is by the design of the advertising itself. We cannot make absolute statements about the superiority of various media. It depends upon your target market. For some markets, flyers could be considered in poor taste and therefore never used by a 'quality firm.' To some markets, direct mail could be 'high class' while to others it could be a nuisance.

So far, it seems that everything we've said about advertising is negative. So what can you do? You must choose the advertising media, timing and location with care; you must approach the design and layout of the advertising with care; and you must get as many people involved in determining the advertising approach as you can. Sales people can be especially helpful since they deal with the customers you wish to reach and persuade. Make sure that everything is consistent with the market you wish to reach and with the image you wish to portray and then, KEEP RECORDS.

Much of the knowledge about what kinds of media, timing, location, design, etc., are effective for a particular business must be gained on a trial and error basis. All advertising is aimed at increasing sales. If it works, that should happen. If something works, keep doing it. If it doesn't work, stop doing it. If you are trying something new, try to add a feature which will make capture of the effectiveness more direct. For example, a new radio commercial might be used which encourages listeners to mention a DJ's name in order to receive a free gift or a special discount. The gift can be a ball point pen with your firm's name emblazoned on it. The point is that knowledge of the effectiveness, or lack of effectiveness, of a particular advertising approach is valuable. A small discount to a customer for clipping a coupon from a newspaper or magazine can be well worth the cost because it will tell you how well the advertisement worked.

With or without some sort of direct measure or feedback of that type, you must have a feel for what the sales should be without advertising in order to judge its effectiveness. That means budgeting. In an earlier chapter we talked about sales forecasting and budgeting. You must develop a history of sales and make forecasts of sales trends in order to determine whether your advertising is having any effect on those sales. Some sort of yardstick is necessary for measurement, otherwise, you will not be able to separate the forest from the trees. Remember the old tale about the security guard who suspected an employee of stealing something from the warehouse? The fellow appeared several times during the day at the gate with a wheelbarrow full of sand for use in the cement mixers and each time the guard carefully searched through the sand. He found nothing, but several days later discovered that more than a dozen wheelbarrows had been stolen. The moral is that the more obvious a thing seems to be, the more it disappears. If you fail to keep careful records, fail to make sales forecasts, fail to use feedback devices, fail to monitor the results of advertising, you can never know whether your money is being wasted.

## ADVERTISING AGENCIES

Advertising agencies exist because the selection of media, timing, location, design and appeal is so complex that many firms prefer to employ professionals to handle the work. Should you consider using an advertising agency? The answer is, maybe. Remember that the primary knowledge required for a successful advertising campaign is knowledge about your target market. No advertising agency has that knowledge. A good agency can have tremendous knowledge about advertising, the kinds and numbers of people who can be reached with various approaches and can have creative people who are capable of outstanding design and layout work. No agency can have a knowledge of your business image or of your operations. That means that if you are willing to spend the time necessary to make the people in an advertising agency knowledgeable about your firm's operation, its target market and image, and if you can find an agency which is willing to spend the time to learn the necessary information about your firm, that agency can be valuable. Without the investment of time on the part of both firms, no effective advertising can be expected to result. The things which an agency can bring to you are knowledge of the advertising business and creativity.

Most of the fees which an agency earns are based on a percentage of media costs. That means that it is possible for an agency to overemphasize the standard approaches of television and radio because those will produce higher fees. Also, advertising agencies vary greatly in skill, knowledge and creativity. They are selling the advertising expertise and creativity of the staff. Consequently, the quality of the service is a function of the competency of the people. If you choose to use an advertising agency, you should be sure that you can develop a relationship with the people in the firm which can be mutually satisfactory. You will need an agency which takes an active interest in your business and is willing to learn about it and its market. You will need an agency which will be open minded about budgetary matters. You will need an agency which is willing to work within your budgetary constraints and is willing to grow with you.

Hiring an agency does not mean that you can stop keeping records. You must still keep records to determine whether the advertising is effective. There is an added factor when an agency is involved. If the advertising is consistently ineffective, you should probably consider changing agencies. In short, it's even more important to keep records when you are using an agency to determine how effective they are in addition to how well various advertising approaches work.

## ADDITIONAL TECHNIQUES

**Marketing techniques** are plans or devices which are designed to sell products or services. Advertising is an example, but is not the only method of promoting sales. Marketing techniques can range far afield from advertising and may result from managerial actions and strategic plans. Virtually anything which has an objective of increasing or obtaining sales can be thought of as a marketing technique.

The approach you take to the sale of goods and services is a marketing technique. Do you use commissioned sales people or salaried; do you use a direct mail approach or have a store; do you use telephone sales efforts or personal calls? There is an almost unlimited variety of **sales approaches** which can be used. From door to door sales to warehouse showrooms; from part time sales people to highly trained professionals; from independent sales representatives to salaried employees; the variety is limited only by your imagination.

How do you decide what sales approach to use? As in the case of the advertising media problem, it is based on knowledge of the target market to which you wish to sell and the image of the business which you wish to portray. You must select an approach which you believe will give you maximum coverage of the market and a competitive position. Frequently, an innovative approach can be valuable because it can make you stand out from your competitors. You must temper your approach with knowledge of the industry. In some industries, the sales approach is so thoroughly entrenched by tradition that it is virtually impossible to change it. For example, college textbooks have traditionally been sold by providing 'examination copies' to professors in the hopes that they will adopt the books for use in their classes. This can be a highly significant expense. Recently, several small firms have attempted to change the sales approach to one which requires a professor to purchase or return examination copies within a certain time if the books are not adopted for use in a class. Many professors have reacted unfavorably to this change because it requires them to review a book quickly in order to avoid being billed for it. That can be a problem given the other demands on time which they experience. Consequently, the firms using the new sales approach are significantly less competitive. Whether a shift in the sales approach will occur over time cannot be predicted as yet. Many other industries have similar traditions which have developed over time and which can limit the success of innovative approaches.

There is another aspect to the sales approach which the customer does not see: the compensation of employees. The sales people can be paid salaries or commissions or some combination of the two. When you are deciding on the sales approach to use, you must also decide on the compensation approach to use for sales people. Generally, when sales people have the opportunity to increase their pay by increasing sales, they can be expected to produce more. Promotions which give away prizes, trips and vacations for achieving established sales levels can be valuable in motivating sales people as can be bonuses and other forms of recognition. The recognition need not always be monetary. In the life insurance industry, for example, top sales people qualify for membership in the 'Million Dollar Round Table' or some other 'club' for high producers. This membership, which may be displayed on business cards, provides recognition and status for excellent performance. Recognition can frequently be worth more than money as an incentive. This is especially true for higher paid people.

We have talked at length about advertising, but we have not discussed its use as a marketing technique. What we mean is the coordination of advertising with operations, conditions and other marketing techniques. How do you decide which items to advertise when you are planning product/service advertising? One approach is to select items which you believe will appeal to the target market at a particular time, i.e., turkeys at Thanksgiving, toys at Christmas, swimsuits in the summer. Another approach is to choose items which are not selling well when compared to other items. Still another approach is to choose items which make you stand out from your competition: items which they do not carry or which are rare or difficult to find. Still another approach is to choose some staple or basic item which has continuous appeal to the market. Yet another approach is to choose items whose suppliers will provide co-op advertising support, which means that they will pay part of the cost of advertising. As you can see, there are a large number of approaches to deciding what is to be advertised. That decision must be made just as the decision about the advertising itself.

In addition, you must coordinate advertising with the rest of the firm's operations. It makes no sense to promote an item which you do not have. If you are experiencing a strike or work slow down, advertising may well be wasted until the problems are settled. On the other hand, if you are expecting a major shipment of some item to come in next week, advertising for that item could be most appropriate. In addition to internal factors, you must also coordinate advertising with conditions outside the firm which could affect it. For example, launching a major advertising campaign the week following large lay offs of people in your target market could be a waste of advertising dollars. In a college town advertising must take into consideration semester breaks and other times when students will not be in town if they are included in the target market. In a farming community, advertising would best be geared to harvest times and could well be affected by extremes in weather.

Other marketing techniques need to be considered as well. Advertising efforts must be coordinated with sales people so that it will assist their sales efforts. In addition, everyone in the business needs to be aware of advertising campaigns so that they can capitalize on those campaigns and so that feedback information about the effectiveness of the campaign can be captured. Advertising must be coordinated with sales and must take into consideration any premiums being offered.

One final word is necessary about advertising. Never overlook the value of the free advertising which comes from '**word of mouth.**' If your customers are pleased with you and satisfied with their purchases, they will inevitably talk about your firm to their friends, neighbors and business associates. If they are displeased with you, they are even *more* inclined to talk about your firm. That means that you should always be aware of the satisfaction level of your customers and strive to keep it high. No advertising which you can buy will be as effective as customer endorsements and nothing can be as damaging to your firm as customer criticism.

## SALES

Everyone understands sales and how advertising is needed to promote sales. What is less obvious are the various reasons for a sale. Sales can be used to get rid of unsalable items. Have you noticed sales items which were marked '**buy one, get one free?**' That sales technique will get rid of more items than simply marking every item down to half price. Another reason for a sale is to attract people into the business. If some items are on sale while others are not, perhaps people can be encouraged to buy some of the regular items. This is the philosophy behind '**loss leaders**' or items which are actually priced below cost. Sales can also be used to attract members of the target market who have not yet become customers or who are unfamiliar with the firm. Still another reason for a sale can be to simply make money. Have you noticed any firms which seem to have a perpetual sale going? As soon as one promotion is over, another starts. Some firms, especially those which choose discount pricing strategies, use sales as their primary sales approach.

If a sale is used for any purpose other than disposing of stale or slow moving merchandise, then you should be aware of the costs and benefits of those sales just as you should be for any other marketing technique. The costs of the sale include the advertising and promotion expense and the lost profits from price reductions. Gains from the sale come from increases in the overall sales of the firm and the profits resulting from those sales. That means that you must compare sales to trends and forecasts as we have discussed in the prior sections. You must be able to tell whether your sales are working or not. Careful record keeping is the only way to make that determination.

We need to make a point about initial sale prices while we are on this subject. If you start a business with a sale, when the prices go back to their real levels, your customers may react adversely. This is especially true if there is a major difference between sale prices and regular prices. Your customers may develop a perception that your prices are higher than the market when in fact that is not so. Many customers are not aware of the exact price of an item, but rather have a *general* idea of its price. When items are on sale in a store which has no history, that sale value becomes perceived as the real value of a product and the return to a regular price is perceived as an *increase* in price. In general, we discourage startup sales for this reason. Customers will generally be curious about a new venture and will be attracted to it simply because it is new. That means that a sale may not be needed for a startup.

## PROMOTION

**Promotion** is more than advertising. It includes signs, layout, point of sale promotional pieces, letters, notes or cards to be mailed to customers periodically, special events and sales, to name a few. Every aspect of your business which is or which can be seen by customers is an aspect of promotion. It is no accident that sales people send their customers birthday cards; retailers send customers private announcements of sales; people in services businesses send newsletters, etc. All of these efforts are aimed at obtaining and maintaining visibility in the eyes of the customer. You want your present and prospective customers to think of your business often and in a positive light. When they are ready to buy, you don't want them to shop. You want them to call you.

Effective promotion requires constant planning. Before the venture is established, you should consider various approaches to obtaining visibility, ensure that they are consistent with the image you want to portray, and establish a time table for their execution. One locally owned furniture store with which we are familiar has a sale every single month. Each sale has a different name and each promises huge discounts off the manufacturer's retail price. The truth is that the store is actually a discount furniture store and the prices offered are those the store would charge anyway. Nevertheless, the sales do work. The store sells the vast majority of each month's volume in the week long sale. Furthermore, the constant exposure from sales promotions makes the store's name a household word.

## PREMIUMS

**Premiums** are gifts, discounts or coupons which are given for purchasing an item. These can range from trading stamps given by a grocery store to dishes given by a bank for new savings deposits. If premiums of any type are used, the advertising should promote the premium offers and should make sure that customers understand the premium program. If customers do not understand the basis for the awarding of premiums, they can become angry and the program can backfire, alienating customers rather than attracting them. In addition, premiums can be costly. Consequently, careful records should be kept concerning the effectiveness of premiums. Added costs of the premium program should be compared to increases in contribution margin which result from the program. Increase in sales is not enough: the increase in contribution margin resulting from sales growth is the profit gained from the program and that must be compared to the cost of the premiums and the cost of any advertising associated with the premium offer. Don't make the mistake of believing that all sales which occur during a premium campaign result from the premium technique. Just as in the case of all other advertising approaches, you must compare sales results to sales trends and forecasts to identify real new business which you would not have received without the premiums. It is even more important in this case because of the added costs.

## BUDGETING

Because no firm has unlimited resources, you must plan how much you intend to spend on marketing efforts. Some firms do this by designating a percentage of gross sales for marketing expenditures. Percentages from 1% to 5% are not uncommon under this approach. When the sales forecast and the expense forecast are prepared, the dollars budgeted for marketing will be a part of the overall budget. Other firms plan marketing campaigns and forecast the actual costs of those campaigns as part of the budgeting process. Still other firms, probably the majority of small firms, do no planning at all and simply spend money haphazardly. There is absolutely no way that any business can expect to maximize the yield from its marketing dollars if it does not budget those dollars and plan where and how they are to be spent.

Once a budget has been prepared, then you must decide how the money is to be spent. That means apportioning the dollars to various advertising campaigns and media and to other marketing techniques. How you decide how much to apportion to each marketing effort on an ongoing basis is largely dependent upon your recordkeeping. The most effective techniques should have the most dollars apportioned. Nevertheless, you should always strive to set aside part of the budget for continued experimentation. The marketing techniques which work are bound to change over time with the changing characteristics of your market, competition and other factors. That means that you must always be trying new approaches. Since the changes will generally occur slowly, it makes sense to spend the majority of the budget on tried and true techniques. However, because change is inevitable, some dollars must always be used to test new and potentially better techniques.

Marketing is the place where every thing in the business must come together. Regardless of what kind of business or industry about which we are talk, its long term success will in large measure reflect the success of the marketing strategy. Every business must sell before anything else can happen. Consequently, every aspect of the business is directed to that end: selling products and services.

## REVIEW

The goal of marketing is to sell goods and services. Advertising is the most visible part of the marketing operation. There are two types of advertising: product or service and image advertising. Product/service advertising is easier to accomplish because the product or service has tangible features, price, and desirability which can be featured. Its primary objective is to create a desire in the minds of customers for a specific item. The risk in this type of advertising is that a demand may be created but satisfied by a competitor. Be wary of making promises which you cannot keep.

Image advertising promotes the reputation of the firm. Its primary objective is to create a specific set of beliefs about the company. Its primary benefit is the isolation of demand to the company. For image advertising to be effective, the image of the company must be consistent.

Media refers to the vehicle used to deliver an advertising message to customers. Besides the usual television, radio, and newspaper, media includes direct mail, billboards, buses, taxis, posters, demonstrations, gifts and premiums, as well as special events and yellow pages. The difficulty arises in the selection of the medium which will provide maximum penetration of the target market for the dollars expended. Timing and location are issues in choosing the medium as well as the content of the message.

Deciding which items to promote is an important consideration. You might choose items with a specific appeal for the season or a basic item which is very desirable. You might select items not selling well, items which make your company distinctive, or items with cooperative advertising.

Tracking the effectiveness of the marketing effort is imperative. You can't really tell whether an advertising or promotion approach is effective without knowing whether your customers actually responded to it. You must also remember the power of word of mouth which can have both positive and negative effects.

Advertising agencies can bring knowledge, creativity, and expertise to advertising campaigns. However, only you can bring the knowledge about your target market, your image, and your products or services to the advertising agency.

Sales are an important technique and are used for a variety of reasons: to get rid of stale items, to attract new customers, to attract existing customers through loss leaders, etc. However, any sale must be tracked to see if the desired benefit actually results.

Promotion is more than advertising. It includes signs, layout, point of sale promotional pieces, letters, notes or cards to be mailed to customers periodically, special events and sales, etc. It includes incentives for employees such as special clubs, recognition and awards for various sales levels. Premiums are promotional techniques which involve gifts, discounts or coupons for customers. To take advantage the various techniques, you need to set a budget and monitor the results of your various efforts.

The marketing effort may well be the most important predictor of success for an on- going company. If you have determined that a business is feasible, then the key is to actually sell your product or service to drive the company to success. To do this, the marketing effort must be well planned, monitored, revised and updated to keep it effective.

# QUESTIONS, EXERCISES AND CASES

**Questions**

1. This is a quote from a well-known individual. Comment upon it and indicate why it is applicable for entrepreneurs. Can you give an example which might support the quotation?

   *It's not the best technology that gets accepted. It's the best promoted technology.*
   *(Thomas Edison)*

2. How is advertising different from marketing?

3. What are the factors involved in the purchasing decision?

4. What is the purpose of loss leaders and premiums in marketing?

**Exercises**

1. Think about the best and worst commercials you have recently seen and indicate whether they are engaging in product/service or image advertising. Which commercials are most memorable and why? Which type of advertising do you prefer and why?

2. Create a marketing campaign for your business. Use flyers and commercials for your campaign. Use a video and/or audio recorder to capture your advertising.

**Case**

Let's revisit the karate school we talked about in an earlier unit.

Randy has commented to us in passing that now things were really going to get hot. "What do you mean?", we ask.

Randy's excited. We had just passed a young man in the doorway and had assumed that he was a supplier of some type, because he was just putting away a check and some papers. Randy was so pleased he had to share his good fortune and we were the recipients of his news.

"I just bought a listing in a directory which is going to be placed in hotels, resort areas and rest areas in a two hundred mile radius! Do you know how many resorts there are in this area? And think of the Blue Ridge Parkway! Business is going to boom now!"

Obviously he was thrilled. We didn't know what to say. We were his customers or at least our sons were and although he knew that we were professors, he had never asked our opinion about anything and seemed reluctant to do more than tell us what he had done and never ask us what he should do.

"Oh, is that the only advertising you're doing?" we asked unenthusiastically.

"Well, you know that the paper carries a special now and then. But it only comes out once at week and I haven't gotten much response from those ads. I have been offering a special, you know, the first two lessons free or a free *gi* with the introductory lessons. I've been alternating the ads. You know, that's a real deal. Those *gis* cost about twenty dollars for the inexpensive ones."

Sensing our lack of enthusiasm, Randy quickly changed the subject and had to go work out with the kids. What could we do? We wanted the dojo to be successful because not only was Randy a great young man, we wanted to continue our boys' studies, not just for the self defense, they were learning, but for the self confidence and self discipline that were already becoming obvious to us. Other parents had agreed with us that while they were glad that their kids were learning to defend themselves, they were more excited about the philosophy that was being taught. Many of us had gone to the karate tournaments and seen the violence taught by the other schools and were truly indebted to Randy for not teaching that type of behavior.

Advertising can be a variety of types as you have discovered in your reading. You can have the soft sell of McDonald's or the hard sell of some of the automobile manufacturers, but you don't need an advertising agency to tell you what appeals to you.

1. Think about this business and what sort of image it wants to portray. What elements would appeal to the most people? Would it be appropriate to ask his students exactly why they had chosen to study with him rather than several other schools in the area?

2. Who is Randy's target market? Why were we not excited about the $150 he had just spent on the directory listing? What is the target market of the directory?

3. Since the newspaper is a weekly paper rather than a daily paper, what other advertising means might Randy have chosen?

4. What was Randy really selling? What is his distinctive competency? Do you think that he knows?

5. Develop a marketing plan for Randy's dojo. Notice that there are two

locations for Randy's business: one is his home town and the other is a college town nearby.

Note: In the home town, there are about fifty percent of the students from the local school systems, mostly junior high students. The other fifty percent are young men and a few young women who are employed in the area. There are several policemen, a couple of postmen, some mill workers, and a few white collar junior or middle managers. In the college town, almost ninety percent are from the university with the other ten percent from the local high school.

Would the same marketing efforts be appropriate for both locations? What would the difference of appeal be in the two locations? What types of marketing would be appropriate in each location? Is Randy adequately tapping the market at either place? What can he do?

6. You have been hired as a consultant. You have been told that there is $250 maximum for the effort. What marketing plans can you come up with? Present your plans to the class.

# CHAPTER THIRTEEN

# E-MARKETING

### INTRODUCTION

The Internet has changed the face of business forever. Any entrepreneur who fails to recognize its impact is unlikely to be able to succeed long term. In essence, the Internet is a new form of *infrastructure*. Infrastructure is the network of systems which support commerce. It is made up of communication systems, including telephones, newspapers, television, radio, magazines, the post office, cell phone systems, etc.; transportation systems, including roads, highways, railroads, postal systems, shipping and package carriers, boatways, ocean shipping systems, etc.; finance systems including banks, insurance companies, finance companies, wire transfer systems, bank clearing houses, monetary systems, etc.; support systems, including sewer systems, water systems, electrical power generation and distribution systems, etc.; and all of the other devices and systems which help businesses to conduct their everyday affairs. In recent years, the Internet has emerged as a new addition to the infrastructure and it has literally changed the business world forever. This chapter examines doing business through the Internet and we will give you some guidelines for harnessing this power to help your business.

## E-COMMERCE

*E-commerce* refers to sales of products or services through the Internet. Recent statistics suggest that about 20% of retail sales are currently occurring through e-commerce. Many people find it more convenient to shop online, or more satisfying for a variety of reasons. This varies dramatically from industry to industry, but think about how significant that number is. If you had been established as a retail merchant for some years, and suddenly you lost 20% of your sales because people started buying the things you were selling over the Internet, you might not be able to survive. That is exactly what has happened to thousands of businesses. As a result most of the *bricks and mortar stores*, as they are called, have had to develop web presences. The advent of Amazon.com, for example, has driven the traditional bookstores like Barnes and Noble to offer their own *web based stores* to try to shore up the sales which they were losing. Most of what we used to call catalog companies have established web based stores now, and many of these use the catalogs that they mail to people to drive traffic to their websites. Many service companies, like airlines, have established web based stores to try to take some of the volume from their telephone operators.

A web based store has a tremendous advantage from a cost perspective because you do not have to employ people to handle the sales process and you do not have the cost of a physical presence. Consider selling a book in a bricks and mortar store. Your first need is to find a physical location and buy or rent a facility. Then you have to stock inventory in that facility and it must be done in a fashion that is attractive to your customers and which helps them to find things in which they are interested. Then, you must employ people to work in the store during the hours in which you are open. Every sale has to be handled by a human who rings it up on the cash register or terminal, and someone must constantly be involved in monitoring the inventory and reordering product. Now, if you have a web based book store, you have to pay for the development of the website and all the software, but this is a one time cost. It is likely to cost less than buying land and building a building, and it certainly will cost less than building a lot of buildings. You may decide to stock some best selling titles in a warehouse, but the vast majority of your inventory may exist only in the form of a listing on your website. Shoppers log on at any time of the day or night, find what they want and purchase it. And, they pay for it at that time, too. You have a much smaller number of people who receive the orders, find the books in the warehouse and ship them, or, place an order to a supplier for the books which you do not have in your warehouse. One person may be able to handle the orders of a hundred people, whereas that would be impossible in a bricks and mortar store. If you are an airline and a customer calls to purchase a ticket, the entire transaction might take 15 minutes, or even longer, as your employee works through the various flight options. If that same customer logs onto your website, he or she can choose his or her own flights and make payment without human intervention.

In addition to potential cost savings, web based stores have another huge advantage: they can draw traffic from virtually anywhere in the world. If you have a bricks and mortar book store, you are unlikely to be able to consistently attract customers who live more than 50 miles away. That means that you must build a great many stores to be able to reach a significant number of people. If you have a web based book store, anyone on the planet who has access to the Internet can log onto your website and buy books from you. You may need to develop multiple language options within your site, but you never have to have more than one web based store.

## WEB BASED STORES

A quick Internet search will reveal hundreds of companies which will provide Internet services for you, set up a web based store for you, design and write the software for you, and in general assist you in starting and maintaining a web based store. There are even Internet Malls which have developed which have a variety of web based stores resident in the same website. These stores pay rent to the Internet Mall, much like you would for a bricks and mortar store located in a physical shopping mall. The costs for these services vary dramatically with the level of sophistication that you might need, but a simple web based store can be started for less than $100 and maintained for as little as $20 per month. Highly sophisticated operations can cost many thousands of dollars to start, of course, and can cost thousands to maintain, but most start up ventures rarely need that level of sophistication. No technical or computer skill is required to establish a web based store or to maintain it. The lack of skill combined with the low cost means that web based stores are within the reach of everyone.

## COLLECTIONS

You will need a company or agent to handle your online sales collections for you. When a small venture is launched on the web, it will generally contract with a company like PayPal to handle its collections. Customers will visit your web based store, make selections of products and deposit these into an online shopping cart, and when they are ready to check out, they will be transferred to PayPal's website. PayPal will take the credit card number of the customer, or the debit card number, or the bank account number for an online check, and process the payment. PayPal will then notify you as soon as it is sure that your money has been collected, and you will ship the order to the customer. You then log onto your PayPal account and transfer the money into your own bank account. Numerous companies offer the same kind of services and the fees that they charge for handling your sales are generally less than you would pay for an ordinary credit card transaction at your local bank.

Credit card sales are not free. The banks and finance companies that issue them charge the merchant a fee for the transaction. This can range from 2% to 6%, depending upon your volume and the smaller your volume the higher your fee. An online collection firm like PayPal may charge you 3%, and it can handle all forms of payment and it removes you from the hassle of calling to ensure that a credit card or check is good. That means that online collection services are generally less expensive than the alternative, as well as less labor intensive.

This process supports the potential for *customer based financing*, which we have discussed in another unit. In essence, your customer pays you first, and you may be able to buy the goods and services which you have to deliver *after* you have collected the money. It dramatically reduces your cash needs when starting or growing a venture.

## ONLINE AUCTIONS

The most famous online auction is probably eBay. This company began by providing a web based store that people could enter and list things that they had for sale. Originally, these were collectibles, or items that people no longer wanted, or casual attempts to get some money out of things that people no longer needed. Interested parties would log onto the website, find the items listed, and make a bid to purchase them. Other people could make higher bids, and so forth, until the item was ultimately sold to the highest bidder. The host, eBay, charged a fee for this service, and the interest grew so dramatically that hundreds of thousands of people were buying and selling items through the auction each month.

As a result of the large number of people visiting the site, other entrepreneurs decided that a permanent web based store could benefit from an eBay link, and now thousands of such stores exist. There are dozens of online auction sites and stores now, many specializing in particular types of merchandise. You can still log onto to eBay to sell things you find in your attic, but you can also set up a permanent business through the website.

A student in one of our classes demonstrated the power of eBay to his class mates during a presentation a few years ago. On the morning of his presentation, he bought a new magazine from a local newsstand that had the picture of a celebrity on the cover. He paid $1.75 for the magazine. During his presentation, he logged onto eBay, listed the magazine for sale, and sold it within 15 minutes for $3.50, and the buyer also paid for the shipping! It turns out that many people in other countries really have trouble finding information about their favorite celebrities. Lest you think the site is only good for small things, another of our students bought a late model sports car through eBay, and many others have paid their ways through college by buying and selling. A number of students were not only able to support themselves through college with eBay based businesses, they left with tidy sums they had accumulated, as well.

## THE NEED FOR A WEBSITE

Everyone needs a website these days, even if you don't actually sell anything through the site. Consider the problem of delivering information to prospective customers and clients. You really can't deliver very much through a traditional advertising approach, but you can always mention a web address. Interested people can log onto that web address and find in-depth information about your business, your services, frequently asked questions, or anything else that you wish to communicate. For this reason alone, having a website to support your venture is almost a must.

Do you need a web based store? If you are selling products, yes. If you are selling services that can be delivered over the Internet, yes. If you are selling services that cannot be delivered over the Internet, probably. Even products that most people will want to buy in person, like automobiles, can be sold over the Internet. As more and more people become comfortable with the Internet, more and more people are likely to develop a preference for online shopping. That means that you will likely need a web based store even if it serves as an adjunct to your bricks and mortar location. You can't afford to lose those sales that will be flowing through the Internet.

Many services can be delivered over the Internet, including accounting, tax preparation, employment services, games and entertainment services, registration and membership services, etc. The list of services which can be delivered over the Internet grows each year as entrepreneurs find new ways of doing business. Even if the service can't be delivered over the Internet, the web based store could still be a good idea. You can schedule haircuts, golf games, arrange for the delivery of groceries, buy movie tickets, make dinner reservations, find a baby sitter, search for the right college, make a dental appointment, and a host of other services right over the Internet.

As is the case with a company selling products, using a web based store to provide services or to arrange for services allows you to employ customer based financing for your venture. When your customer makes an appointment, he or she must make a deposit. That is cash up front before your services are delivered. It drives down the cash required to start your venture and makes growing your venture easier.

## E-MARKETING IN OPERATION

Having a website or a web based store also opens additional advertising options for you. This is what we call e-marketing and it includes both traditional advertising support, and internet based advertising. Consider using billboard advertising. The viewers of the boards are driving past and are occupied with the process of driving, so they cannot give much attention to an advertising message on a billboard. However, if you feature a website prominently on a billboard, and it is an easily remembered website, catching your prospective customer's attention is dramatically eased. A few short words to peak interest and a website address can drive interested customers to your site to learn more about your offerings. On the site you can present a complete and in-depth message and hopefully move your customer to a purchase.

Your company does not even need to be a web based store. Let's say that you are running a tourist based business targeting parents with young children. You have built a petting zoo, a Christmas store, a souvenir shop, a candle making operation, and a toy and doll store. You have a huge range of entertainment options, but you cannot convey your offerings on a billboard. You could buy six billboards and feature part of your operation on each one, but that not only costs six times as much, some of your message is lost as people miss one or more boards, and fail to connect you with all of the various messages. Now, use a brightly colored board with a short message like, "Children's World: Making Magic for Children," and add an easily remembered website like, www.ChildrensWorld.com. Color pictures of animals, Santa, toys, etc can add visual interest, and parents with small children can use their cell phones or notebooks to log onto your website for location, maps, pricing, venues, etc. That's e-marketing in action!

In addition, e-marketing opens up a host of new advertising and marketing opportunities on the web, itself. You can arrange for links to other websites that prospective customers might frequent, pay for various types of ads on various websites, or advertise in a variety of ways on the Internet. In addition, your website will be available to the various search engines as people go online to find goods and services like those you supply. Many of these search engines will arrange for your website to appear in a short listing or on the first page of search returns for a fee. Some of these may be significant, but if you are selling goods or services that are hard for people to find, paying a search engine for a high placed listing might be the best marketing dollars you can spend.

This is especially true if you are specializing in really unusual collectibles. Let's suppose that you have a passion for collecting umbrellas. With a web based store, you can turn that passion into a real business possibility. You can provide historic information for collectors and feature the rain protection treasures that you have found in yard and estate sales, as well as modern contributions of sun protection popularized in New Orleans. Increasingly, people turn to the Internet to find rare and unusual treasures and with the right search engine placement, you can be there to satisfy their demands.

## BRICKS AND MORTAR STORES

The final question which might come to mind is, "If the Internet is so great, do I need a physical store at all?" For many ventures, the answer might well be, no, or, at least, not all the time. Of course, if you want to operate a restaurant, the web based store might be problematic. Although, you might find success in a virtual restaurant that taught dining etiquette. We have a friend who sells Halloween supplies, costumes, and novelties. As you might expect, this is a highly seasonal business. He found early on that he really could not justify the cost of a year round physical presence, so he started a web based store. He now sells year round to a large number of clients out of the country who buy his products because they are novelties. Can you believe that people in Transylvania really want to buy fake blood? Each year, he rents a kiosk in several shopping malls, and sets up a physical presence for the month before Halloween. He now sells more through his web based store than he does through his physical kiosks, and in recent years he has cut back on the number of kiosks he operates. Last year, he only rented one kiosk, and it was his best year ever.

Many thousands of entrepreneurs have launched ventures in the last few years that have no physical presence at all. Many others started with a web based store and later expanded into a bricks and mortar store. The costs to launch a web based store may well be far less than to launch a physical store. The costs to operate a web based store may also be less than the cost of operation of a bricks and mortar store. These combine to potentially create a lower break even point for your venture and/or to make it more profitable at a lower level of sales.

If you will be selling goods or services that do not have broad based appeal, the web based store becomes another viable option. If only a small percentage of the population will be potential customers, then having a web based store makes that small percentage potentially very large. Remember that umbrella store? Unless you are located in a really major metropolitan area, you might find that not enough people collect umbrellas in your market area to make a business based on that activity viable. On the other hand, even if the percentage of interested people is quite small, your web based store could be viable because it has the potential to be available to the entire world. There's bound to be lots of umbrella collectors in the world, don't you think?

## REVIEW

*E-Commerce* refers to sales of products or services through the Internet and recent statistics suggest that about 20% of sales are currently flowing through the Internet. This is being driven by increasing numbers of people who find it more convenient or more satisfying to shop online.

A web based store has a tremendous advantage from a cost perspective over a physical store. It can cost less to launch such a venture and it can cost less to operate it. In addition, it can give you an opportunity to literally reach the entire world with your venture. One of the most powerful aspects of a web based store is its ability to support customer financing.

With a quick Internet search you can find hundreds of companies which will provide Internet services for you, set up a web based store for you, design and write the software for you, and in general assist you in starting and maintaining a web based store. You do not need technical knowledge, and the costs are generally quite low. Collecting money is actually easier, less expensive, and quicker over the Internet than it is in a physical store. Many service companies provide collection services, and one of the better known of these is PayPal. Online auctions were made famous by eBay and hundreds of thousands of people sell things they find in their attics, collectibles, and an amazing variety of things on eBay each month. The auction has attracted so many people that thousands of entrepreneurs now operate web based stores linked to eBay.

Everyone needs a website these days, even if you don't actually sell anything through the site. *E-Marketing* refers to the facilitation of communication with prospective customers, and web based support for advertising. It is also important to have a website for people to find through search engines, as this is becoming an increasingly popular way for people to learn about everything.

If you can deliver goods or services over the Internet, you most likely will need a web based store even if it only operates as an adjunct to your physical store. Many entrepreneurs find that a web based store is all they need. Such a venture may well cost less to start and operate and that drives down the breakeven and drives up profits. In addition, a web based store can reach people all over the world, turning an operation which has a very small level of attraction into a potentially viable venture.

# QUESTIONS, EXERCISES AND ASSIGNMENTS

## Questions

1. Define the following terms:
   a. infrastructure
   b. e-commerce
   c. bricks and mortar stores
   d. web based stores
   e. collections
   f. online auctions
   g. customer based financing
   h. web presence
   i.. e-marketing

2.` What are the advantages and disadvantages of web based versus brick and mortar stores for a restaurant? For a book store?

3. How does one get paid from online stores?

4. How does a web presence differ from a web based store?

5. Respond to the comment: "If the Internet is so great, do I need a physical store at all?"

## Exercises

1. Visit the internet and notice web based stores such as Amazon.com and E-bay.com. Notice what is sold and how. Notice how products are bought and sold.

2. Do a web search for the number of sales being made on the internet this year. How can one not have a least a web presence to direct traffic to a business.

## Case

Mary had a wonderful concept. She wanted to make coats for chefs; actually female chefs! Having graduated with a degree in culinary arts, she had tested her skills in a number of fine restaurants and earned her chef designation. However, she had been constantly frustrated by the uniforms she was expected to wear. Mary was a extremely attractive young lady, but the uniforms chefs were expected to wear were designed for the male physique. Not only were they uncomfortable for women, they were singularly unattractive.

Having just entered a graduate entrepreneurship program, Mary was tasked with coming up with an idea for a business as part of her coursework, she decided rather than starting her own restaurant which was somewhat cost prohibitive at this point in her life, she would design and sell chef outfits for women. She and her friend designed and sewed a variety of form fitting and very attractive outfits. Now she needed to decide how she would sell them.

Creating a retail store in her area was problematic as she was from a small town where the unemployment was over 12 % and there were few fine restaurants. Even had she lived in a large city, she needed to reach a large geographic area because of the scarcity of chefs, and therefore, the limited size of a potential, physical market. She decided that she needed to sell over the internet. This was a perfect solution for her since the startup costs were minimal and the potential was wonderful because she could theoretically reach all the female chefs in the world!.

She began her process by having a photo shoot with all of her new outfits, then hired a web designer to set up the site. She is now finalizing her web presence and eagerly awaiting her first order.

1. Do you think that this was the best decision based upon the circumstances?

2. What are other ways that she might promote her site?

3. Should she create a retail space as well? Why or why not?

4. What other things might she sell through her website?

5. Determine what costs might be associated with her startup?

# CHAPTER FOURTEEN

## MARKETING STRATEGY

### INTRODUCTION

Thomas Edison, the *wizard of Menlo Park* and one of the most prolific entrepreneurs and inventors in American history, understood how to introduce a product to the market. Between 1870 and 1880 when he introduced his light bulb, he frequently explained that the *best promoted* technology could beat the *best* technology. Today, we see that happening all the time. That's because most of us really do not have the knowledge or experience to be able to identify one product or service as technologically or inherently superior to another. Rather, we rely upon what we are told and that means largely on promotional information. Edison did not just invent things. He built companies and businesses to build and market his inventions. He did *not* license anything, he created ventures to produce and sell everything he developed. Edison knew that each of his hundreds of products was faced with copycats, immediately after they were released. Each of those releases was also rapidly followed with improvements, enhancements, and superior technologies from a host of other companies, building on his innovation. As a result, he paid a great deal of attention to promoting his products and to convincing the public that they couldn't live without his inventions. In fact, at least one biographer called him the *publicity wizard of Menlo Park.* If you would be a successful entrepreneur you must follow Edison's lead and devise strategies that will draw people to you.

## MARKET PENETRATION

Regardless of how exciting your vision, and regardless of how vital is your venture, you must still devise a way to penetrate the market. That is, how do you intend to attract your initial customers, clients or patrons? How do you intend to beat the competition? Not only must you devise a strategy, you must be able to describe it and write about it in your business plan. Unless you are like the restaurant owner who opened his venture in a small town, all of whom watched the construction with great curiosity, you must do something to get your target market to recognize your existence. In some retail cases, an initial clientele might be guaranteed, but even then retaining that clientele is a different matter, as our restaurant owner rapidly learned. Further, identifying a strategy can be the secret to success. Frequently, this is a matter of creativity.

A few years ago, we had a client who had developed a highly sophisticated software system that would allow a user to determine how much money he or she needed to save based upon the kinds of investment strategies available and considering the target income level for retirement. Our client had set up a website, and literally invested several millions of dollars in trying to get people to log onto the website and purchase the services. Nothing worked, and the client was failing.

When we looked at the problem we recognized that the issue was one of market penetration. People who are interested in utilizing a software product like that are people who are actively involved in investing in some sort of retirement or pension plan. That means that there is really not a significant market for the product because there are so few people engaged in that activity.

We suggested converting the product into a private label solution for commercial clients. Our client embraced that strategy and converted the website to emulate a commercial client, then targeted small banks and investment companies with a direct sales approach. That is, they identified small investment companies which were handling 401k funds for clients, then used sales agents to approach those clients. The idea was based on the belief that these institutions would have clients interested in this kind of software, but would not have the technological capability to develop a similar package.

The sales agents offered each of these institutions a private label solution. In essence, our client would customize a page in its web site for the institution's clients. For example, tf you were the Southeastern Pension Fund, your clients could log onto your web site and click on a tab which would allow them to work with a sophisticated planning system. The look of the page and the operation of the system preserved the belief that it was a Southeastern Pension Fund system. In reality, the clients would be working within our client's web page. The price was extremely low: just a few pennies for each client for each month.

Within the first few months, the software firm had sold two institutions which together generated over a million dollars in annual revenue. With these clients in hand, selling others was easier and our client branched out to look for institutional clients nation wide.

In some cases, the demand for a product or service is so great that nothing more than the most basic of promotions is required to penetrate the market. One of our former students started a venture like that.

Our student owned a tract of land in a rural county and was trying to determine a use for that land which would produce a continuing source of retirement income. The dozen acres constituted a picturesque site and featured gently rolling hills. It was far from any town, but it did have ready access to a four lane highway connecting the county to Interstate highways.

After a broad based research effort, she determined that the county was home to more than a dozen campgrounds, all of which boasted 100% occupancy during the camping season. She visited each camp ground and carefully identified their strengths and weaknesses and verified that each of them turned away patrons, many of whom traveled another 50 miles before finding a campground vacancy.

She built a campground on her own land, taking care to include improvements over the existing competitors that she had visited. These included better spacing of the parking areas, careful attention to the view that each camper would enjoy, and the layout of a roomy bathhouse She placed a single billboard advertisement on the four lane highway. Before the first week was over, she had a dozen campers, four of whom arranged for year round, permanent parking of their recreational vehicles.

As you can see, the demand was so great that little promotion was required for the market to discover the existence of the venture and the billboard ad was an effective market penetration strategy. However, you should note that the single, four lane highway was the only such road in the county and was the principal thoroughfare. That meant that every camping prospect passing through the county, or traveling to any of the competing campgrounds would see that billboard. We worked with a client who bought a campground in a neighboring county to hers. That client experienced quite different results.

Our clients were a married couple in their late fifties who had purchased a campground which they hoped would constitute their retirement. It was a beautiful place located deep in the mountains and far from any city. Having been avid campers for thirty years, our clients knew the market well and they knew that there were literally dozens of campgrounds in the county, all of which filled up during the camping season. This campground was a little run down as it had been shut down for the last four years, but our clients were confident that a little sweat could put it all to rights, and they erected a large, full color billboard on the highway at the entrance to the campground.

After the first disastrous year, they were nearly out of business and they were completely out of money. They had never attracted more than a handful of campers throughout the season and they wanted our help in finding money to support the venture through the winter and to complete repairs and renovations.

Can you guess the difference between the two campgrounds? There really was a huge market demand in both counties, but our second client was located on a highway which was not well traveled. The main thoroughfare in this county was miles away and few prospective campers passed the billboard they had erected. The moral of the story is that an entrepreneur must devise a strategy for penetrating the market based on the circumstances of the venture, its market and its area.

## COMPETITIVE ADVANTAGE

There is always competition, if not competition for the products or services your venture will offer, then competition for the dollars your venture will try to collect. The question which we must answer, and be able to support in writing, is how we will establish our venture and take market share and revenues from the competition. Have you read about the so called dot.com debacle? Hundreds of ventures were able to obtain venture capital funding to launch web based businesses. Their stock values soared while analysts were continually decrying the absence of any underlying financial strength which could support such stock price growth. People investing in and financing these firms expected them to revolutionize markets ranging from donut sales, to lingerie, to travel planning, to prescription drug sales, to toys, to children's clothing, to... Well, you get the picture. In essence, thousands of people thought that these companies would change virtually every market for goods and services in existence. Then, the bubble burst, and the vast majority of these firms went out of business, producing huge losses for the venture capitalists and investors.

What happened? People, many of them quite knowledgeable under ordinary circumstances, lost sight of the fact that the Internet was simply a factor in the infrastructure. In order for a venture to succeed, it must be based upon a vision which incorporates an understanding of how the market can be penetrated and how the venture can gain competitive advantage. Customers, clients and patrons do not award their business to a venture solely on the basis of its sales and distribution approach, regardless of the evolution of the infrastructure. They give their business to a venture because that venture has sound strategies for attracting their attention and for beating the competition, both initially and on an on-going basis. In the excitement over web based businesses, entrepreneurs and investors forgot those basic principles.

We had a client who had built a successful food ingredient business on relationship selling over the last 25 years. That is, he represented companies that sold flour, sugar, spices, butter, etc., and negotiated sales of these items to commercial clients like bakeries which needed these ingredients. His sales agents had been calling on the purchasing agents of the commercial clients for years and built strong relationships with those buyers. However, our client saw the handwriting on the wall and understood that this approach was doomed by the Internet. Commercial buyers would shortly be able to find what they needed with a brief Internet search, and would not require an agent to find the supplies. In essence, the evolving infrastructure would destroy relationship based, business to business operations.

Our client chose to proact by establishing a web site which would support food ingredient buyers in posting anonymous requests for bids, and food ingredient sellers to respond with anonymous bids. He planned to attract business by certifying the capabilities of both buyers and sellers and by developing software which would allow both parties to accept direct input of the results of the transaction into their respective accounting systems. His web site not only expanded access of both buyers and sellers from a few dozen firms to the entirety of the world wide market, it saved time, and dramatically reduced costs for all participants.

However, being an experienced entrepreneur and a student of business, he realized that establishing a web based venture was no different from a bricks and mortar operation. He still had to devise strategies for beating the competition, both initially and in the future. He knew that he had a serious deficit in that his brokerage firm had a very limited number of clients, both on the supplier side and on the buyer side. That is the nature of relationship marketing. It involves intensive relationships, but because of that intensity, the number of relationships is typically small. However, among the attractions of a web based brokerage business would have to be a large source of both suppliers and sellers. There would be little advantage that his web based brokerage would have over a strong relationship broker unless he could offer both faster and cheaper service AND a large range of contacts.

Consequently, our client began a campaign of attracting venture partners from among his competitors. Within six months he had recruited 12 partners, each of whom was operating a traditional brokerage firm in competition with his own. Each of these businesses would bring to the new venture all of its contacts and the new firm planned to systematically convert each of those relationships into initial clients for the web based business. At the same time, strategies called for a systematic recruiting effort aimed at contacting every food ingredient supplier and every buyer in the United States within the first year. International suppliers and buyers were targeted for solicitation in the second and subsequent years.

As you can see, this entrepreneur understood market penetration and competitive advantage. By bringing in a large number of his former competitors, he seemingly reduced his own potential returns from the venture. However, this process ensured his success as it provided him with a start-up field of buyers and suppliers that no competitor in the industry could match. Now, he could offer the lower costs and faster service times that the web makes possible, but, he could attach that service to the more important opportunity to vastly expand supplier and customer bases for clients of the firm. Not only that, but he put into place an action plan which identified and targeted food ingredient suppliers and buyers throughout the country. Each of these businesses would be introduced to the new venture and recruited to the network of clients. Each new entrant not only raised the commission levels for the venture, but increased the size of the network which made the operation that much more attractive to future clients.

Not every client with whom we have worked devised such elegant strategies. We were retained to prepare a business plan for another web based business which had a very different perspective of how to penetrate a market and gain competitive advantage.

Our clients were avid golfers and had evolved a vision of a web based venture that would provide a wide range of services to golfers. They had raised some initial capital from among their personal circle of friends and relatives, and now they wanted to refine their vision into a business plan which they could use to approach venture capitalists.

The vision for the operation involved providing golfing news to web site visitors. The leading competitors for this kind of operation attracted 750,000 to 1.2 million unique visitors per month or more and our clients thought they could garner a share of that market. Revenues would be based upon advertising. The golfing market is an attractive one for advertisers because it represents a more affluent group, consequently, advertisers would be easily attracted to a site that could boast a large number of golf enthusiasts.

Our clients planned to offer a host of services similar to those offered by the competition. These included weather forecasts, the opportunity to book tee times at virtually every golf course in the nation, reports and evaluations of new equipment, golf pro stats and line ups for tournaments, as well as golf news and sports news in general. They realized that none of these services made the venture unique or helped it to stand out from its competitors, so they devised a strategy to differentiate the firm.

Our clients would run a 24/7, on-line, raffle. Every hour, some user, currently logged onto the site, would win a prize. Each day, a user who had visited the site that day would win a prize. Among those golfers who made the web site their home page and visited regularly, one would be selected each month, each quarter, and each year, to win larger prizes. The prizes would range from golf balls for the hourly prizes, to golf clubs for the monthly prizes, to a golfing trip visiting and playing the top 12 golf courses in the world for the annual prize.

Can you contrast the strategies of the two clients? The first based his strategy on a sound understanding of the demands of the markets and the limitations of the competition. He devised an approach which would provide his venture with immediate and important competitive advantages. He offered clients the broadest list of contacts, and the cheapest, and the fastest transactions in the industry. His longer term strategies included expanding and retaining that initial advantage.

The second clients based their strategy on offering the same services as their competitors. They intended to gain competitive advantage through offering the chance to win prizes. We had serious doubts about that strategy on two fronts. First, the competition was well established. The leading golf web sites had been in business for several years. Taking market share away from those firms seemed to us to require a stronger and more basic advantage. Further, a contest is a simple thing to duplicate. Should the strategy prove successful and attract patrons, competitors could easily respond by offering their own contests and take those patrons back. We encouraged our clients to devise a more lasting strategy, but they were convinced that their vision was sound. We completed the business plan for them, but they were never able to attract venture capital funding.

The moral of both stories is the same. Crafting a strategy which can penetrate a market and gain initial competitive advantage requires an understanding of the market and the strengths and weaknesses of the competition. Hopefully, the entrepreneur gained this knowledge through the venture planning process because the prospects for the venture are only as strong as the strategies it develops. Remember, the idea may be 'insanely great,' as Steve Jobs, Apple co-founder, was fond of saying. That does not mean that success is guaranteed. The idea has to be promoted, as Thomas Edison taught us. In fact, in our experience a weak idea, or even a poor idea, effectively and strongly implemented has a better chance of success than does a great idea which is poorly implemented.

## INDIRECT COMPETITIVE ADVANTAGE

What about the case of a venture which will only have indirect competitors? Remember that indirect competition is competition for the dollars your clients, customers, or patrons will spend.

Developing strategies which will establish competitive advantage in such a market requires a creative approach. You need to be able to answer several questions, and your venture planning hopefully addressed these points. What kinds of things or activities currently consume your target market dollars? Why do these things appeal to your target market? What can you do to establish a greater level of appeal?

One of our former students evolved a vision of a retail operation which would offer candles, decorations, Christmas items, collectibles, and souvenirs to the tourist trade. She selected a market area in which no such retail operation existed, therefore, she faced no direct competition. Nevertheless, she recognized that her indirect competition was high because a large number of retail operations competed for tourist dollars.

Recognizing that attracting tourists was largely based on opportunity, she selected a site which was highly visible and easily accessible, and situated on a major tourist thoroughfare. In close proximity was a large number of other retailers also seeking to appeal to tourists. This assured the shop of the opportunity to piggyback on the traffic flow generated by the concentration of shopping opportunities. Now, she needed a reason for tourists to stop at her shop.

Tourism clients in her market area were dominated by families. Recognizing the role that children play during a family vacation, our student installed a petting zoo outside her shop. The visibility of the animals and their appeal to children would drive business to the shop. At the same time, she pursued wholesale opportunities and established a network of other retailers who wanted to stock her candles in their own stores.

Her strategy was successful because she understood her target market motivations. Family vacationers are attracted to child-oriented entertainment opportunities. Note that our student also devised a strategy to capitalize on the very competitors against whom she competed by converting as many of them as possible into wholesale customers. Success in that approach involves a well-planned direct sales effort and an excellent product. She had established a manufacturing process for the candles which produced a wide variety of scents and colors. This made them appealing to many retailers as the candles made attractive additions to displays and stores through their eye-catching colors and their pleasing aromas. Her direct sales approach was to call on each retailer before the tourist season began with a demonstration kit of colorful candles.

Another of our students also launched her own business. In this case, it was a surprising kind of venture. She wanted to establish a venture in her home town and she lived in a rural county, but she was not sure what kind of business might be successful. After considerable reflection, she settled on a fishing pond. Having lived in the area for many years, she knew that fishing was a popular past time in the area and that many of the residents enjoyed trout fishing in the streams of the county, while others would make infrequent fishing trips to distant areas where major lakes could be found. That made her believe that a fishing pond had potential. Her research in the county revealed that there were no such ventures, in fact, not even any similar ventures, but she knew that she still faced competition from every other form of entertainment available in the county.

The target market consisted of local residents, a large majority of whom had limited disposable income because the county was relatively poor. To succeed, she would need to establish a significant repeat clientele, and that required a strategy which would consistently produce advantages over other types of entertainment available.

Despite her familiarity with her home town, our student engaged in a research activity to identify indirect competitors and to devise a strategy for defeating them. She quickly learned that during the Fall, the major indirect competitor was high school football. She also determined that no alternative form of entertainment was likely to defeat that. In fact, a large number of the residents followed all of their high school sports, and many traveled to neighboring counties to follow and cheer their teams at their away games. There were no bowling alleys or other forms of organized entertainment for miles, although there was a local movie theater. Its patronage seemed surprisingly low, until one considered that the movies were relatively expensive for a poor populace. In fact, the teenagers of the county gathered in the evenings in the parking lots of local businesses and visited with each other. A drive through the county on a Friday night would reveal large numbers of pickup trucks parked in small groups in one parking lot after another.

Our student decided that she needed an inexpensive entertainment, one that could consistently beat the prices of all the alternatives. Her research led her to the idea of stocking her pond with catfish. Catfish are extremely resilient. They are easily caught, but if released, they will survive, and even thrive. They grow rapidly and fight strongly. Consequently, she established a low hourly charge and admitted children accompanied by an adult free of charge. To this she added a buy back plan. Patrons could sell back the fish they caught. These would be released in the pond thereby reducing the cost of restocking. In addition, cash prizes were offered for the largest fish of the day, week, month and year. The local newspaper readily agreed to photograph and print pictures of these winners together with their catches. Penetrating the market initially was simple. She placed a large sign on the road in sight of the location for the pond which predicted its completion date and included its pricing. By the time the pond was finished, everyone in the county knew it was under development.

As you can see, this entrepreneur concentrated on learning how to create a demand and gain competitive advantage which could be sustained. Her vision was of a low cost entertainment which appealed to the local clientele because of the fishing tradition which existed in the county. Her venture provided family outing possibilities in a county which had a strong tradition of supporting its youth, as evidenced by the enthusiasm for high school sports. Her choice of venture, catfish fishing, allowed her to minimize her costs so that she could sustain low prices, and her arrangement for publicity created a constant, free source of advertising while providing additional appeal to her clientele, each of whom greatly desired to be the featured fisher.

Not every story is so successful because a lack of direct competition can mean that there is simply an inadequate market to support the venture. One of our former students developed a vision of establishing a bowling alley and entertainment center in her home town. There were no such facilities in the county or the town, which had a population of about 7,000 people. She intended to offer pool, snacks, a baby sitting service, bowling leagues, contests, etc. She did a great deal of research and refined the vision to that of an extremely attractive facility. However, the cost of such a facility mandated either high prices, or a high volume of clientele. Her venture planning convinced her that high prices were simply impossible in the face of the inexpensive entertainment alternatives available, and that the population of the area was inadequate to support a high volume. Her efforts remind us that sometimes there is no direct competition in an area for a very good reason.

On the other hand, the absence of direct competition could simply mean that no one else has thought of the venture. Another former student of ours also wanted to start a business in his home town. He liked where he lived and he wanted to stay there, but there was little industry and few jobs. He researched the various possibilities for a venture and evolved a vision of a dry cleaning and laundry service. There was no such service in the town or the county. He was initially concerned that people chose clothing which could be washed instead of dry cleaned and that would make him unable to compete with the indirect competition of the home laundry. However, his venture planning convinced him that a significant number of people did prefer clothes which needed his potential services. These people seemed to be minimizing their cleaning requirements and periodically utilizing the services of a dry cleaner in an adjoining county when their business or shopping took them there. Further, our student reasoned that a local dry cleaners might encourage people to buy clothing that they would ordinarily not purchase. To make a long story short, he built the dry cleaners and within a year was well established and growing strongly. Three years after establishing the venture, he has hired a full time manager and seldom visits the shop. He has gone on to establish additional businesses on the strength of the cash flow the dry cleaners has provided.

## SUSTAINING COMPETITIVE ADVANTAGE

We cannot leave the topic of strategy without discussing the issue of sustainability. A *sustainable competitive advantage* is one which your competitors cannot overcome. That is, the advantage can be maintained in the future and continues to give the venture an edge over other direct and indirect competitors. Traditional management textbooks talk about sustainable advantages a great deal, and the concept is immensely appealing. Develop some strategy or some aspect of your venture that the competition cannot equal and cannot challenge. Such a strategy would ensure the success of the venture into perpetuity.

Clearly, that idea is absurd. There is no such thing as an advantage which is always sustainable. Anything that you do that is successful can be, and probably will be, duplicated eventually. That is the nature of entrepreneurship. Entrepreneurs are always searching for new and better ways to do things. Your venture is likely to be a victim of those searches if you persist in believing in the invulnerability of the competitive advantage which you established when you started. You need to interpret the phrase, 'sustainable competitive advantage,' as 'temporarily sustainable competitive advantage.'

In fact, attempts to create sustainable advantages has led to major problems in dozens of industries. You hold an example of that in your hands. We produced this book as a *trade book* deliberately to avoid the problems inherent in the college text market. How did the rising and often absurd prices of college texts develop? It developed through well-intentioned people seeking competitive advantage without consideration of the long term effects. Years ago college texts resembled trade books. They were bare-boned efforts with an attention to price. Then, publishers seized on an approach to the market in which they developed ancillaries to make teaching the book easier. At first, these consisted of instructor manuals, test banks, and the like. These were given to instructors who adopted the book, and the cost of the ancillaries was added to the price of the texts. Before long, other publishers duplicated that approach, and the ancillaries began to become more sophisticated. Competitors responded, and books began to become more expensive: glossy paper, color, photographs, etc. At the same time ancillaries became more expensive: full color transparencies, videos, etc. The result was rapidly rising costs and a trap for any publisher who tried to break out of the mold. If you stop producing ancillaries, or if you cut back on the cost of the text, you are now at a competitive disadvantage because the market has been trained to expect these things.

The textbook price spiral illustrates the problem with competitive advantage. Like most things in business, it can have two sides. If you establish an advantage that works, then you will take market share away from your competitors. They cannot tolerate that, so they must respond, and they must respond by duplicating or surpassing your advantage. When they do, that strategy which used to provide advantage becomes a basis of competition. That means that all of the competitors in an industry must provide this concept to the market because the market has been trained to expect it. It no longer gives anyone an advantage; it is now required just to stay in the game; just to remain competitive. No one can back away because that would mean a loss of market share. Further, if these attempts at creating competitive advantage drive up operating costs, then the firms in the industry are trapped in a situation in which they cannot reduce their costs. The only choice is increasing prices until the market finally rebels, or until some entrepreneur comes along and finds a better, cheaper way. In the case of textbooks, that is likely to take the form of digital books or web based books, but clearly the current approach is doomed.

The moral of the story is to be careful how you decide to differentiate yourself. You must establish a competitive advantage or you will never penetrate the market. On the other hand, you must be careful not to develop a strategy which simply costs more money and is easily duplicated. That will do nothing but ensure that your advantage will be fleeting and that your costs will be constantly rising. We had a student who wanted to start a fashion venture aimed at producing clothing for college students.

Our student had recruited an entrepreneurial team which included two other individuals who were talented fashion designers. Together they had developed an avant garde line of clothing targeted at the college market. Their plan was to arrange for manufacture of the clothing overseas, and to distribute it through a limited number of retailers appealing to the college market and having stores located close to major universities. They planned to wholesale to these stores through a combination of push strategies consisting of direct calls, and pull strategies developed through a concentrated marketing program targeted directly at the college consumer.

To establish a competitive advantage, they planned to recruit college athletes at major universities. Just as shoe companies promote their products by encouraging professional athletes to wear them, our student entrepreneurial team intended to give clothing to college athletes with the expectation that their designs would become highly visible and desirable on campus.

To maintain their advantage, they intended to continuously develop new styles, and to continuously lead the evolving sense of fashion on college campuses. They planned to develop a brand identity and to establish that brand as being at the forefront of youth fashion.

As you can see, this approach relies on repeating the design successes of the original venture and in maintaining an active sense of college fashion trends. In essence, it means reinventing the firm every year. Since the makeup of the target market changes every year, and the college athletes in favor change every year, it is a constant effort to recruit new models, to attract new consumers, and to set new clothing trends. All of these were concepts that the entrepreneurial team found immensely exciting.

So, how do you establish an advantage that truly is sustainable? You do it through entrepreneurial vision. The development and refinement of the vision is an on-going process. It never ends. This is why it is so prevalent for firms who force out their entrepreneurial founders in favor of professional managers to ultimately lose their competitive advantage: they lose the ability to evolve the vision. What we want to do is substitute *sustainable vision* for sustainable advantage. An entrepreneur must continuously engage in venture planning; must study the market and market potential as it evolves and its needs and interests change; must observe the actual and potential competitive environment as it develops and matures; must maintain an awareness of actual and potential resources and infrastructure. The vision for the venture must change with changes in the environment, preferably on a proactive basis. If that happens, each new refinement of the vision will be coupled with a new identification of strategies and new competitive advantages. It may even be that the new vision involves abandoning past products, services or markets, or building on those to take the venture in an entirely new direction. Entrepreneurship is not a singularity and a vision is not the sudden switching on of a light bulb. They are processes and that's what makes it so fascinating and so much fun. It never gets old or dull because it is always changing.

**REVIEW**

With Thomas Edison's statement that the *best promoted* technology beats the *best* technology every time, we understand that having an outstanding product or service is not enough. We must be able to let others know we have it and create a demand for it. No longer is the story of the *better mouse trap* true. While is it possible to find that mouse trap today, it still must be promoted. The *beaten path* is not automatic.

So how does one go about letting the world know what you have? For established firms it may be as simple as advertising, But for a new venture just opening its doors, how do you attract your initial customers, clients or patrons? How do you beat the competition? Not only must you devise a strategy, you must be able to describe it. It must be real and doable. We call this strategy, *market penetration*, and it often takes much more than just advertising using the traditional media. Remember the same strategy does not work for everyone. You may have to be creative.

There is always competition, if not competition for the products or services your venture will offer, then competition for the dollars your venture will try to collect. The question which we must answer, and be able to support in writing, is how we will establish our venture and take market share and revenues from the competition whether it be direct or indirect. Market penetration with *indirect competition* is a bit harder than with direct competitors as there are no direct comparisons possible.

A *sustainable competitive advantage* is one which your competitors cannot overcome. That is, the advantage can be maintained in the future and continues to give the venture an edge over other direct and indirect competitors. Clearly, this notion is absurd. *Temporary sustainability* is possible, but cannot usually be maintained into the future. The reason, of course, is that if an advantage can be created, it can almost certainly be copied, which means that your one time advantage becomes a *basis of competition* for the industry and everyone adopts it. Now the advantage is no longer yours, but you must continue to employ it. Think of the recent attempts by several companies to raise revenue by charging fees for the use of debit cards. Expectation by the consumers is more important than trying different strategies which attempt to change accepted norms

Entrepreneurship has often been called a roller coaster ride. It is thrilling as the company grows and is successful, but it often is frightening as the coaster starts its deep descent. Being able to plan for the future is an ongoing process, but it will even out those deep descents and help the ride to stay exciting.

# QUESTIONS, EXERCISES AND ASSIGNMENTS

**Questions**

1. Define the following terms:
   a. best promoted
   b. market penetration
   c. competitive advantage
   d. indirect competitive advantage
   e. sustainable competitive advantage

2. Explain the following statement by Edison:

   *It's not the best technology that gets accepted. It's the best promoted technology.*

3. Most marketing texts teach you about how to budget for the marketing of products and services for large companies which already exist and for which there is already a market, but how do you market the products or services for a new business which is just starting?

4. What is competitive advantage and how does one achieve it?

5. It is usually much more difficult to take market share from indirect competitors than from direct competitors. Explain why this is so.

6. Why is it a fallacy to say, "A *sustainable competitive advantage* is one which your competitors cannot overcome. "

7. What often happens when the entrepreneur is replaced by a professional manager?

8. What happens when a competitive advantage becomes a basis of competition?

**Exercises**

1. Look at existing companies and list those in which they have the "best promoted" product or service, but they do not have the "best" product or service. What often happens to the company which has "best" product or service?

2. Look at examples in which competitive advantages have eroded into bases of competition. What happened to those companies and why?

**Case**

Doug and Carl came to see us about starting a business to see if we could write them a business plan. Carl had worked for twenty years as a painter in a high end community where houses were sold at one million dollars plus. He had been very successful as a subcontractor.

Now his son, Doug, was about to graduate from the local college with a business degree and wanted to go into business with his Dad. Carl had virtually run his own business as a subcontractor, but he had never had to keep the records he would now.

The pair decided that they would open a wholesale and retail shop selling paint as there was not one close at hand. The supplies for the paint crews working in the area come from the nearest large town which was two hours away or through other onsite suppliers. If an individual wanted to paint a house, Walmart would have to do.

After discussing the project with the pair, we assigned them the task of finding some data for us before beginning the plan. We needed to know the costs and expenses associated with their venture. Initially they wanted to build a new building on a piece of land accessible to the two main roads in the county which was for sale. However, they could lease a building not far away as well, so we could do the calculations both ways.

We also needed to find out how many housing starts there were in the county and for what priced homes. With Carl's experience and Doug's business degree, we felt that perhaps this venture could be successful and agreed to take the job.

1. Do you think this venture could be successful? Why or why not?

2. What the advantages and disadvantages inherent in starting this business?

3. Does the state of the economy affect your decision? Why or why not?

4. How should the pair go about penetrating the market to ensure clients?

5. Do they have a distinctive competency and is it temporarily sustainable? Why or why not?

# INDEX

Made in the USA
San Bernardino, CA
20 February 2018